THE GREATEST BILLY COTTON BAND SHOW

The *Greatest*
Billy Cotton
Band Show

By JOHN MAXWELL

JUPITER · LONDON

TO MARIA

Who, throughout all the preparation of this book,
has cheerfully and patiently kept my evening meal for me
more times than I've had hot dinners.

First published in 1976 by
JUPITER BOOKS (LONDON) LIMITED
167 Hermitage Road, London N4 1LZ.

SBN 904041 31X

Copyright © John Maxwell 1976.

Composed in Monophoto Bembo Series 270
and printed and bound in Great Britain by
Butler and Tanner Limited, Frome, Somerset.

Contents

Author's Note and Acknowledgements

I HAVE experienced the greatest possible enjoyment in writing this book. I have had a richly rewarding time renewing acquaintance with Billy Cotton's great bandsmen and singers, and the pick of the scores of stars who were delighted to appear on the Billy Cotton Band Shows. I should like to thank my friend Allen Andrews for the accuracy with which he has remembered, sometimes better than I, so many graphic conversations with the great star of the show himself, our old friend Billy Cotton.

Further thanks are also due to Bill Cotton, BBC Head of Light Entertainment; Leslie Grade; L. G. Woods and Alf Dewdney of EMI; Miss Kathie Kay; Alan Breeze; Eddie Gurney; Tony Frewin; Brian Tesler of London Weekend Television; Liz Rezler of the BBC Photograph Library; Ronnie Waldman; Richard Willcocks; Richi Howell. And also a special word of thanks to Terence J. Price and many more too numerous to mention.

John Maxwell

[vii]

Bill Cotton produced the TV Band Shows
before going on to become BBC Head of
Light Entertainment.

Foreword by Bill Cotton O.B.E.

WHEN I WAS ASKED to write this foreword to *The Greatest Billy Cotton Band Show* my first thought was to use that old, worn-out cliché of despairing compères – 'And now I'd like you to meet someone who needs no introduction'. However, on reflection, I realized that as well-known as my father was, there were still many facets of his character and career that the general public didn't know.

The Greatest Billy Cotton Band Show portrays him as he was – a warm, generous entertainer who had the 'common touch' and also an enormous respect for his audience and fellow professionals. He had a great entertainer's unique ability to make his audience forget the trappings of stage or studio, and to enjoy themselves with him, because he was one of them. But behind his relaxed warmth was the sheer professional – a man who had learned his business the hard way. He set high standards for himself and expected those he worked with to aim for the same standards.

My father knew and counted as his friends stars from all walks of show business, and many of them appeared regularly on the Band Show. But it wasn't just the big-name artists who featured on the shows – he discovered and gave opportunities to many unknown performers.

Here in *The Greatest Billy Cotton Band Show* you can meet them too – the established stars and the performers he discovered and helped to stardom.

I know that my father is still remembered with great affection by many people. I hope that this book will bring to them yet more happy memories of Billy Cotton and his Band Show.

THE GREATEST BILLY COTTON BAND SHOW

Billy Cotton at rehearsal for his 150th TV Band Show.

'WAKEY·WAKEY'

BIG BAND, BIG SOUND, BIG PERSONALITY, BIG BUSINESS. COMEDY, glamour, spectacle, and tunes, tunes, tunes. All the richness of the British variety stage channelled at some time or other through one master entertainer. That was the Billy Cotton Band Show. That *is* the Billy Cotton Band Show, because it still remains a vivid and colourful part of life for the millions and millions of us who enjoyed it. We cannot look back on the show without a warm smile of affection for the man. But, much more personal than that, there is also the warm recollection of *ourselves*, the happiness we knew, the affection we shared when we took our own part, through so long a section of our lives, in the Billy Cotton Band Show. Billy Cotton made people feel better then. He makes them feel better now, just by going back in memory to the good old times.

For forty wonderful years there was a Billy Cotton Band Show, and what you have in this book is the chance to choose your best memories of your own lifetime. Almost every entertainment star in the firmament was glad and proud to appear with Bill. They are all here, in this book, reminding us perhaps of 'our tune', our best laugh, our private happiness, our moment of glamour, away from all the workaday problems of the ordinary world.

So let's dive into this rich revival of our past happiness.

Remember how the television shows used to start? Always some crazy gimmick, leading up to Bill roaring, 'WAKEY-WAKEY!' Remind yourself

1

Billy Cotton and Harry Secombe always made
a superb comedy duo.
DAILY EXPRESS

2

of the good old days with a gander at this typical script by Jimmy Grafton, who wrote winner after winner in unfaultable continuity for the Billy Cotton Band Show. Settle in your seat. You know the programme is going to be good. On the bill with That Man and the Band are Harry Secombe, Matt Monro, Mrs Mills, Alan Breeze, Kathie Kay, the High-Lights, the Leslie Roberts Silhouettes, and the Rita Williams Singers. You know it's going to be good. But what twist are they going to use to start it this time?

Ah! They are fading up on a weather chart. Who's that coming into shot with thick, horn-rimmed glasses? Harry Secombe, of course. He's speaking with a very heavy Welsh accent. And while he talks he turns back to the weather chart to put in a line or two.

'Good evening,' Harry is saying. 'I just thought we'd have a look at tomorrow's weather now. Pretty miserable really, isn't it? Let's see what we can do to improve it, like. An anticyclone here ... a couple of areas of low pressure there, and there ... a dry westerly breeze coming in from here ...'

As he is putting in the lines on the weather chart, you see that what he is really doing is a very good drawing of Billy Cotton's quite unmistakable face.

'And that's what I call a really bright outlook,' says Harry, stepping back from the chart.

You're looking at the chart, with the lines showing Billy Cotton's face, and gradually the chart melts into the face of the real Billy Cotton, held by another camera and superimposed on the chart.

And what does Bill do? Why, exactly what you'd expect him to do. His hands go up on each side of his mouth, and out comes that well-known roar that assures us we're all sitting pretty again for another enjoyable show:

'WAKEY-WAKEY!'

The band comes tumbling in with the roustabout strains of 'Somebody Stole My Gal', that deathless tune which is Billy Cotton's signature. Bill is smiling with that old cleft-potato grin. There's a bustle about the stage, but first Bill makes his usual casual announcement – never, ever pompous, just off the cuff and to the point:

'Well, with Harry Secombe getting together with us later on in the show the outlook certainly is bright. Meanwhile, where are those Silhouettes?'

Those gorgeous girls are all round him now, hustling him – but what bloke would object to being hustled by the Silhouettes? The script progresses:

Bill: Now, what shall we play for our opening number?

3

SILHOUETTES SHOUT VARIOUS TITLES.

Bill: Just a minute! Who's boss around here?

Silhouettes (*dutifully*): You are!

Bill: Right! So listen – we'll play 'em all. But, to start with –

FADE IN BAND – PLAYING INTRODUCTION.

Bill: 'Let's Get *Together*'!

And in a great swirl the music is belting and the girls are dancing and Bill is singing and the girls are coming back at him with every other line. They switch in and out of the four tunes. Bill leads the words as the tunes change. The girls back and echo him. They all come together in the last three lines of the lyric of 'Side By Side', and then the band crescendoes to take the music alone with a strenuous thirty-six bars of non-vocal while the girls are dancing their routine. And there's Bill, dancing with them. Cor, that man is light on his feet. The cameras cut and climb and track. There's Bill with the three lines of girls. Now there's a side shot of Bill footing it with the four girls in the front line. Bill's stepping it backwards and the other two lines of girls are coming forward and the lines cross. The music changes from quickstep to eight bars of cha-cha-cha, and the camera tracks in to get a full-length shot of Bill and two of the girls cha-cha-cha-ing like crazy. Back to quickstep, side-shots, cut and climb, the formation is getting tight and suddenly they are all singing again as the camera takes a full shot of the dance and its precise finale.

A gale of applause sweeps up and this is no phoney, that dance was worth all the beef that's being put into those hand-claps. A camera is closing in on Bill. You wonder how he's got the breath to speak, but he's not troubled, and his announcement is as short and to the point as ever: 'Well, that's sorted that out. Now here's a return visit from a young man who was recently voted among the first five male singers in a poll held by American disc jockeys, and that's pretty good. So we are very pleased to welcome him tonight, and here he is with his latest recording, "Softly as I Leave You" – Matt Monro!'

Matt Monro sings his number with the band, and as the applause comes up again everybody who is anybody knows that the next item is the elaborate comedy number that the Billy Cotton Band Show always puts on in number three position. Who are they going to kid this week? We're not left long in suspense, because Bill is already making his announcement:

'Now a lot of people are rather sad that a certain detective series is off the air for the time being, so to ease their disappointment we're going to give you our musical version of an episode. It might give you a clue to which

Billy Cotton with the Leslie Roberts
Silhouettes.
BBC COPYRIGHT

5

Billy Cotton took to dancing late in life but was praised for his routines with the Silhouettes. Here he is seen doing an impersonation of Harry Champion.

series it is when I tell you that of the fifteen songs we use, fourteen are either French or French-type – so pull up your chairs and get ready for a bit of mystery and suspense.'

So it's going to be 'Maigret'. Jimmy Grafton always lets himself go superbly in these intricate comedy sequences, and the versatile members of the Billy Cotton Band Show invariably turn up trumps. While the band plays creepy music we see Michael John of the High-Lights, dressed up in drag as a caricature of a '*vairy* Parisienne' woman – asleep. A shadow passes across his face. You can see a club descending on his head. The 'lady' jerks up with his eyes open and crossed in what the professionals call the 'commercial headache' effect. The camera cuts to a spoof of the normal 'Maigret' opening scene, with Rupert Davies's shadow on the wall and then the detective striking a match. But the title-caption that goes on the screen is not 'Maigret' but 'Migraine'. This French detective is to be Inspector Migraine – and judging by the after-effects of that club, 'Migraine' is going to be an under-estimate.

The band is playing Ron Grainer's genuine 'Maigret' theme, but the picture (trust Jimmy Grafton) is going wrong. Alan Breeze – 'Good old Breezy', as Bill Cotton calls him – is playing the Inspector, but he can't get his match to strike to light his pipe. An unidentified female arm appears in shot and supplies the light!

Then, with the band backing him, Breezy goes into one of the fifteen parodies of well-known songs which the script-writer has provided for this comedy number. The tune is unmistakably 'Pigalle', and the words go:

> I'm Inspector Migraine, French police's best brain,
> That's the talk down the Rue Pigalle.
> I spend all my time solving crime after crime
> As I walk down the Rue Pigalle.
> I'm the strong silent type, so I fill up my pipe
> And I smoke away
> I can't stand the stuff, but it's useful to puff
> When I find I've nothing to say.
> Everyone is impressed as I make an arrest
> When I've walked down the Rue Pigalle.
> But it's all so easee when it's all on TV
> As you walk down the Rue Pigalle.

Two of the band come on to do a spot as Migraine's assistant detectives, and Rita Williams arrives in a preposterous get-up as Madame Migraine.

7

To the tune of 'Love's Last Word Is Spoken' she warbles:

> You forgot your breakfast, Chéri.
> You *could* have had a peck first, Chéri.
> I've brought you some cognac and saucisson.

In reply Alan sings:

> Please go or you'll bring my neurosis on.

And then, 'Saucisson!' he exclaims, pushing her away and out of shot.

The plot continues outrageously. The 'Parisienne' who was clubbed in the first shot, tries to explain the assault to Migraine, singing to the tune of 'Why Does My Heart Go Boom?':

> Boom! I was in bed when Boom!
> A club on my head went Boom!
> Boom, boom-bedy-boom, trying to kill me.

The comedy roars on. Migraine comes to a locked cupboard in her bedroom in which he declares the attacker must be hiding. When the door is forced, out stagger three old men, Billy's veteran bandsmen – Frankie Kenyon, Laurie Johnson, and Bill Herbert. They are sent off to jug, and as the final captions roll Migraine pinches the girl who offers again to light his pipe, takes out a club from underneath his coat, and says 'We shan't need this any more' – thus indicating that he was the attacker all the time. As 'The End' appears on the screen, a further caption follows, which reads: 'Next Week – The Man Who Got Locked in the Louvre.' And another of the show's inimitable comedy numbers is over.

Billy Cotton announces the next number, a song by Kathie Kay. Thanking her afterwards, Bill says, 'Well, what with the Silhouettes, Rita Williams, and Kathie Kay in the show, you'd think I've got enough feminine company. But I'm a glutton for punishment, so once again here's our keyboard Cleopatra – the Jezebel of the Joanna – Mrs Mills!'

Mrs Mills plays a couple of numbers and then swings into 'You Must Have Been a Beautiful Baby', which Billy Cotton sings with her. Then some of the boys from the band come front stage at Mrs Mills's invitation to back her in another tune. She light-heartedly christens them 'The Mills-Tones', but they're far too accomplished to be Millstones round anybody's neck. They are Grisha Farfel on trumpet, Jock Reid on tuba, Ray Landis with washboard, Laurie Johnson and Bill Herbert on banjo, and Billy Cotton himself wielding the sticks. They do a very catchy version of 'When My Sugar Walks Down the Street', and they are immediately followed by the

Billy Cotton with two of the Cotton Singers
from the 1968 series of Billy Cotton's Music
Hall

Silhouette girls in a big production number dancing to eight consecutive tunes and yielding one vocal to the High-Light boys.

At the end of the production number the girls are left in a close huddle. But they suddenly start screaming – obviously something is wrong. Bill Cotton comes on asking officiously, 'Here, just a minute, what's going on there?' He dives into the group, the camera following him, and, hey presto, it's Harry Secombe at the heart of the bevy of beauties.

'What's the idea of making your entrance like that?' demands Bill.

'Can you think of a better way?' ripostes Harry. 'Don't be angry with me, William,' he pleads. 'Tonight let's be gay and forget our cares' – and he seizes Billy Cotton in a purposeful dance grip and asks, 'Do you come here often? How about doing the Twist?'

Secombe is only deterred from finishing the Twist – and possibly finishing Cotton in the process – by being ordered to sing. He sings straight, 'Girls Were Made to Love and Kiss' by Franz Lehar. Then he starts off in hot pursuit of the Silhouettes again. But Bill Cotton stops him and reminds him they are down to sing a duet. After some argument in which Bill rejects a couple of operatic suggestions they sing 'The Army and the Navy' with the full band. There's plenty of comic business with bugles that don't blow and motor-klaxons that do, and after a tremendous tussle the turn ends with an elaborate film effect in which, after an explosion, Bill and Harry catch an American rocket as it is falling to earth. 'They won't like this at Cape Canaverel,' says Harry.

It looks like the end of the show but, as usual, there's one more surprise.

'Wait a minute, Harry,' says Bill as Harry is retiring after the applause, towards the girls. 'There's something I've always wanted to do.'

'If it's dangerous, don't let me stop you,' says Harry.

'Will you let me conduct my band while you sing?' Bill asks.

'What,' says Harry, 'and see who finishes first?'

'No, I'm serious. How about "Bless This House"?'

'Well,' says Harry, 'if you're game, I am.'

'Right,' says Bill, 'you announce it.'

As Bill takes up his position for conducting, Harry announces, 'Ladies and gentlemen, "Bless This House", and may the best man win.' And the show comes to a fine conclusion with Harry singing in his best voice.

HOW THE BAND SHOW BEGAN

By sheer professional experience Billy Cotton had set the formula for the Band Show quite early in his career as a showman. Hundreds of Billy Cotton

Band Shows were broadcast on the radio and television, and because he was reaching millions of people at one time, he could not repeat any performance. Every show had to be original and different, but the difference had still to be contained inside the formula that Bill had worked out. In addition to this, of course, there were literally thousands of Band Shows given on music hall stages, or before huge gatherings of troops in war-time, where the great warm personality of Bill came through at its most valuable pitch in maintaining the morale that kept our boys cheerful.

Billy knew all about keeping up morale because he had served as a youngster in the First World War. He was born on 6 May 1899, enlisted early by falsifying his age, and went on to have a very active life in his youth. As he himself said, 'I had my pilot's wings before I had ever earned more than six shillings a week in Civvy Street, I was racing motor-bikes on my meagre First War gratuity, and I was playing League football full-time before I had my first band.'

William E. Cotton was born in Smith Square, Westminster, the youngest of ten children. His father was then a turncock, a man who had to turn the water on whenever there was a fire. 'In those days they couldn't have a fire without my father,' Bill used to say. Mr Cotton's headquarters were the Rochester Row fire station. If the fire was handy and local, he would start off on his own as soon as he got the alarm, and beat the firemen to the blaze. But if it was some distance away he rode along with the others on the horse-drawn fire-engines. He was at one time bandmaster to the Chelsea Water Board.

Bill himself never touched an instrument until he joined the Boy Scouts. 'The 1st City of Westminster was a great troop,' he recalled. 'After regular Sunday church parades we would form up outside and march round the streets, then very proudly down Victoria Street. We had a lovely drum and bugle band. I never had time with the troop to qualify for the drums, which were good – and loud. When I went on the bugle my mate, Fred Thatcher, used to tell me, "Blow up, Cotton, because we can't hear you with the drummers in front."'

By the autumn of 1914 Bill was in the Army, at the age of fifteen and a half. He had volunteered for the London Regiment (Royal Fusiliers), and nobody asked his age. By New Year's Eve, 1914, he was in Malta. He now had his drum as well, for his rank was drummer-bugler. After a few months he did further training in Egypt and landed at Gallipoli to take part in the hopeless battle for the Dardanelles. He landed in the middle of an artillery barrage, and as he lowered himself into the water to wade ashore a marine threw him a rifle, neatly cancelling the significance of the bugle badge on Bill's sleeve with the remark, 'There's only one bloke blowing a horn tonight. That's Gabriel, and he's up in Heaven. And you'll be bleeding-well with him if you don't catch hold. *Catch hold!*'

Bill was in the front line right through the rest of the year into the freezing winter, only coming out when the whole expeditionary force was evacuated. He had been recommended for a commission in the Royal Flying Corps, and he worked his passage to Blighty as a stoker in a battleship. While he was waiting for his flying training he qualified as a gym instructor on a course in the Army Gymnastics School at Aldershot. Finally he got to Yatesbury and learned to fly Bristol fighters. He flew solo for the first time on 1 April 1918, the day the Royal Flying Corps became the Royal Air Force, and he was still under nineteen years old. He did some pioneer flying-boat work, making experimental landings on water in a DH6 equipped with floats, which was intended to be used for submarine spotting. But he crashed a Bristol fighter while showing off with some low-level manœuvres, went into hospital for four months, and by the time he came out the war was over. They asked him to stay in the RAF, but he took his gratuity and left the service.

Jobs were hard to come by in 1919. Bill did one spell as an acrobat in a music hall act after one of the partners had knocked himself out with an injury, so his first public appearance as an entertainer was tumbling round the London circuit of halls like the Metropolitan, Edgware Road, and the Kilburn Empire. He was boxing for the London Polytechnic and playing football for Brentford in the Third Division of the League. And he earned a little money by playing the drums in a scratch dance band called the Fifth Avenue Orchestra. Most of the time they were playing only on Saturday nights, and the average money earned for a gig was thirty shillings. In the middle of that not very stable existence he married Mabel Gregory at Christmas 1921, and they set up their first home in two rooms in Kilburn Lane.

Bill practised the drums religiously, but he couldn't get much work. Then his nephew, Laurie Johnson, got him a few band jobs. Laurie's father had married Bill's eldest sister, and though Laurie was Bill's nephew he was only four years younger. At eighteen he was already something of a dance band impresario, which shows the sort of progress people made in those days. 'Laurie played the fiddle, which was a sight more easy to carry around than my drum kit,' Bill used to say. 'He and I were always very fond of each other, and that friendship has lasted right through our careers.'

Bill got a job 'on the buses' as a conductor working from Cricklewood

Drummer-Bugler Cotton, W. E., 3065, of the
London Regiment (Royal Fusiliers).

13

Team photo of Brentford. Billy Cotton is
sitting third from the right.

14

Garage. He bought the best set of drums he could obtain – and Laurie said that when they went on a gig no one could get on the stand because of the space they took up. 'There was even a set of bells,' Bill recalled, 'which is the secret reason for a number called "American Medley" being played to death by the band in its early days – because it had a part specially written for the bells.' Laurie secured an engagement at the Ealing Palais de Danse, seven nights a week including the private Sunday Club, and brought Bill into the band full-time. Bill stuck to the buses, wangling it so that he always took an early shift. Then, when the great Wembley Exhibition opened in 1924, Laurie won a contract to play every day in what they called the Palace of Dancing. Bill went too, and still tried hard to keep his job with the bus company. Unfortunately, one day the garage superintendent decided to take his wife to Wembley. 'Being fond of a one-step, he took her into the Palace of Dancing. Being interested in the music, he studied the band. Being familiar with his bus men, he decided that he had seen the face of the drummer before.' Bill was fired from the London General Omnibus Company.

There were lean times when Wembley closed in the autumn, but Bill got a Christmas job at Olympia. Then he had the chance of an audition with the musical director of the cinema circuit that was eventually bought by Gaumont-British. This time Bill took the initiative and persuaded Laurie and three others to go along for the audition. They had only ten tunes in their repertoire, and they were on the tenth before the musical director said he liked them and offered them an engagement at the Regent, Brighton.

The date was 1925, and Bill had his first band ever, which he called the London Savannah Band. He moved down to Brighton for the engagement, taking his wife and his young son, Ted. Laurie Johnson went with him, playing fiddle, and he engaged three others for piano, trumpet, and saxophone. They became popular at Brighton, because they were a very nice band to dance to. They played 'Tea for Two', 'I Want to Be Happy', old musical-comedy stuff, and American hot numbers. They used to buy small orchestrations by stylish American bands through a contact man who would meet the liners at Southampton and collect the numbers from a courier. But Bill Cotton did not get on very harmoniously with the management of the Regent, and very soon he was snapped up to lead the resident band which opened the Palais at Southport on 29 May 1925. Laurie Johnson did not go north, but went to lead his own band at Dreamland, Margate.

Shortly after he opened at Southport, Billy Cotton – still leading the London Savannah Band from the drums – heard that three old acquaintances wanted to join him. Bill introduced them to the Southport audience in what

Billy Cotton's first band, the London Savannah
Band, at Southport in 1925.

A formal photograph of the band in the late twenties.

he called 'my first bit of stagecraft and showmanship'. He went out onto the floor and made an impressive announcement: 'Ladies and gentlemen, I brought a good band to Southport Palais, but I always planned that three lovely players whom I am now going to introduce to you should join it, because now we are going to be wonderful. They are Sid Lipton on the fiddle, Joe Ferrie on the trombone and a beautiful singer too, and Clem Bernard, a superb pianist. They are three boys whom I used to work with before I came here. I have always said that if only I could welcome them to the band we should have the finest band in the world. Now here they are, and here we come!' The spotlights were grouped on the middle of the floor, and the three bandsmen came in playing, Clem with an accordion. They played 'Marta', and they were superb. The crowd rose to them. The spotlights followed them as they went up on the stand and they sat in with the orchestra. This marked the beginning of their long association with Billy Cotton.

Clem Bernard was to become Bill's lifelong friend and right-hand man, on whom he could put total reliance. Billy had a funny reminiscence about Clem's arrival in Southport. 'I had great faith in Clem's musical judgement, and I first asked him to listen to our sound from a balcony during the session. Afterwards I asked him what he thought. "Well," he said, "the sound is quite good, but you'll have to change the drummer." I said, "Well, that's a bit of cheek for a start, since I'm the drummer. What do you suggest that I do?" "If I were you, I'd stand out in front and conduct," he said. "You saucy beggar," I said. "Anyway, how do you feel about it? Do you want to join?" "Yes, I think so," said Clem. "Well, you can have a week's trial," I told him. Thirty-three years later I asked him how long he had been with me. He told me, and went on, "You gave me a week's trial, but I'm still waiting to hear whether I got the job or not."

'He was a marvellous person, and I loved him,' Bill said of Clem. 'He was a little Scot with a hunched back, and he was very sensitive about his appearance. He was my musician, and apart from his work as the pianist I gave him all the arrangements and the technical responsibility for the performance of the band. He was a real musician.

'When we developed into comedy he took no part in the music hall knockabout we used to indulge in. But when the second war came and many men had to leave the band I asked him if he would join in the comedy routines. He was very nervous that people would laugh at him as a hunchback, but he turned out to be a natural comedian, greatly loved by his audiences. Clem and I had a wonderful relationship. Professionally I was absolutely dependent on him. And he virtually died in my arms. He was conducting the band at rehearsals for a broadcast. Suddenly he said to me, "I feel giddy." I said, "Well, get down, you silly so-and-so." "I can't," he said, because he had to stand on a high box to conduct. I lifted him down, and as I held him he collapsed. Shortly afterwards, somebody said to me, "You've lost the best servant you ever had." I said, "He was never my servant, only ever my partner." A week later I sang "Smile" on the radio show for Clem Bernard. And I wept.'

Under Bill's direction Clem Bernard rehearsed the London Savannah Band into rock-hard rhythm. They used to stay up night after night until three in the morning to listen to what they could pick up on the primitive radio of those days broadcasting the music from America.

'We were a strict-tempo band,' Bill used to recall, 'a *dance* band. We were the first over here to recognize the importance of light and shade in music. We made a band sound nice to dance to – imaginative.

'We got a pretty good name. The railway company used to run special trains – what they called Dance Expresses – to bring dancers to Southport from all over the North. At that time I decided to leave the drums and stay out in front. With Clem on the piano we had become a terrific blues band, and Clem and I took it further. When the band went off for a rest, just Clem and I used to stay, playing the blues. I used to sing through a megaphone, because there were no microphones then. Clem and I used to carry on, with me singing perhaps thirty songs a night – all blues. The floor was packed. They loved dancing the blues. Southport was the greatest blues audience I ever saw.'

During Billy Cotton's great stint at Southport between 1925 and 1927, he introduced several dances absolutely new to Britain. At that time dancing was taken very seriously – people *enjoyed* dancing well and expected their partners to dance well – but it was also regarded as great fun. In addition, it was something of a status symbol to master new dances fast – which is why the Black Bottom came first to Southport, Lancashire, of all places in Great Britain, rather than to the very chic Society dance clubs of the West End of London. There is no better person to tell the story than Billy Cotton himself.

'We were playing the afternoon session at the Palais. Suddenly I saw a middle-aged man and woman standing in front of each other and occasionally bumping their backsides together. My eyes nearly fell out of my head, and all the boys in the band were laughing. We were playing a rumba at the time.

'Scandal! Suddenly I saw that the couple had been ordered off the floor.

19

During the break the manager came over to me and asked me down to his office. "They are very nice people, Bill," he said. "I've not thrown them out. He is an American with his wife. They don't mean any harm. He says he likes the band here, but why don't we get up to date and play the Black Bottom?"

'I was introduced to the American. He said to me, "Sir, this is a craze in Manhattan at the present moment. They have special nights at the Starlight Roof devoted to the Black Bottom. They ask the Negroes to come on and do it. I'm a great enthusiast, and if your pianist will listen to me I'll sing him the tune."

'I said, "Will you wait until tea-time?" and I got hold of little Clem. The American went through it, and very soon Clem too knew the Black Bottom. He knocked out an arrangement which helped keep us all together, and that night we *played* the Black Bottom. The American came for the evening session, and he danced it with his wife. He brought the house down.'

Southport was the cradle of Billy Cotton's great show business career. Here he became a success, and here he formulated the philosophy which sustained him throughout his life. 'I got a satisfaction out of seeing people enjoy themselves to my music. If they didn't, I felt there was something wrong. And that taught me my greatest lesson. Music gives more pleasure than any other branch of entertainment I know.

'It was at Southport that we made our debut as a stage band. We took a cinema and we put on a band show, which was really the first exploratory step towards the big band shows of ciné-variety in the thirties. The experience certainly changed my outlook. My thoughts became more and more concerned with presenting a band as sheer entertainment. In any stream of change in one's life, often presenting itself more clearly when one looks back over the distance of years, there always seems to be one small factor which has been a constant presence in all phases of the change. In my case the factor on this occasion was the fascination I had for the music of Gershwin's *Rhapsody in Blue*. I played this at my first stage show in Southport, and when, much later, I was occupied with stage band shows exclusively it was for a long time one of my standards. After I had broken into gramophone records I made an ambitious recording of *Rhapsody in Blue*. There was controversy about the making of it, but when I played it to Paul Whiteman, who was in England for a show at the London Hippodrome, he said, "That is the most inventive record I have ever heard." The secret of it all was something that is an old trick now, but at the time it was novel and effective. I knew the sound I wanted, and discussed it with Clem. There were instru-

Clem Bernard performs a comedy number
while Bill watches.

21

ments, particularly in the woodwind – oboes and clarinets – that I didn't have in the band. I said to Clem, "Let's get in this fellow Reginald Foort." (He was then playing the organ at the Grange, Kilburn.) "The organ can take the cues for the instruments we don't have." And we made the record like that, with the organ fattening the band for the *Rhapsody*.'

After his successful stint in Southport, Billy Cotton was appointed musical director for all the dance halls of the General Theatre Corporation. Besides doing administrative work in Birmingham and Liverpool, he conducted his band at the Astoria in London's Charing Cross Road. At the Astoria, Bill recalled, 'a surprising number of people never seemed to dance at all. The floor was much smaller than what I was used to, and there was a tendency always for a crowd to form by the band, just standing and listening. They just used to listen and ask for more: "Go on, Bill, play 'Bohemia' ... play 'Tiger Rag'." They always had to station commissionaires to keep the crowd moving away from the front of the band.'

In a financial merger, the General Theatre Corporation was taken over by Gaumont-British, who had already acquired the circuit of which the Regent, Brighton, had been part – and W. E. Cotton was in management trouble again, since the management with whom he had not seen eye to eye at Brighton was now his immediate boss again. He moved to the Locarno, Streatham. He was now billing himself as 'Billy Cotton and his Savannah Band'. 'I was enjoying myself, and I think people were enjoying me,' he later recalled. 'In the summer I was asked to do many of the College Balls at Oxford and Cambridge. I have dance cards for that time still. They still had dance cards then, with the programme printed and a space against each dance to note down the partner you had booked it with: they even had a little pencil on a silken string dangling from the fold. I notice that we played mostly foxtrots or Yale Blues. "She's Funny That Way" was one of the blues, and among the foxtrots were "Lover Come Back to Me", "I'll Get By", "You're the Cream in My Coffee", "Blue Moon", "Broadway Melody", and "The Wedding of the Painted Doll". When we talk about "standards" and "evergreen" songs of the past, perhaps we forget that they are not a great sifting from decades of tunes. All these songs were current within the space of a year or two. You might say that people knew how to write songs then, and the public knew how to appreciate them. But you certainly don't need any *excuse* for the way in which these golden oldies kept cropping up in the Billy Cotton Band Show. They had earned their mileage.'

Bill next took an engagement at the exclusive Ciro's Club, an appointment which was hailed with great surprise by the musical journals. According to Bill, 'They forecast that I would be there for twenty-four hours, or just long enough for me to open my mouth. And certainly when I went in and saw the reaction to my sounding brass, I thought we would be out the first night. I had a very good team: Nat Gonella, Joe Ferrie, Sid Buckman. We draped half our wardrobe over the bells of the trumpet and trombone and made a nice quiet sound. We had to play quietly because it was a very select place. They didn't want to hear the band, only feel it. They didn't want to be disturbed while they were telling a "funny" to the girl, or eating and drinking and shooting all the lines imaginable. For the first two or three nights even we talked in whispers, we were so overawed. I had a hard time getting people to go onto the floor and *dance*, and when they did they used to act very snobberoo, going round as if they had a smell under their nose.

'It was probably true that my personality did not fit in with the place. Especially on account of the fact that I was never willing to bow to the members, even, I am afraid, to the Prince of Wales, who was a constant client. The managers used to say to me, "The band is magnificent and, Mr Cotton, you are a very nice man, but you must remember the members expect a little courtesy." "Courtesy!" I said. "You mean servility, and I'm not servile to you or Lord Muck." "But when members come in," they went on, "why don't you bow a greeting to the guests? It won't hurt you." I said, "I know it won't hurt me. And I'd do it if I didn't think I'd look a burke doing it. I don't do that sort of thing, because I wouldn't know how to. I don't mind saying 'Good evening' in the proper manner. But there will be no bowing and scraping from this side of the stage."'

'The band is magnificent,' the club managers had said, and now the whole of Great Britain began to be aware of it. In 1929 Billy Cotton began his first regular broadcasts from Ciro's. The first radio transmission in which Cotton had been heard occurred long before there was a British Broadcasting Corporation: from the old Palace of Dancing at Wembley Exhibition in 1924, where an engineer shunted in a 2LO microphone and the band let blast at it without any balance or control. But now, in 1929, discreet late-night dance music from posh clubs was considered a highly sophisticated polishing of the BBC image, and Billy Cotton was a BBC favourite. It helped him in his power struggle with the music publishers, who had always been sticky about allowing him to use the numbers they bought from America, but now saw that he could do them more good than they could

23

Billy Cotton was a pioneer of radio, and
broadcast regularly from Ciro's, the exclusive
nightclub.

deprive him of if he broadcast their tunes to the listening millions. And there *were* millions – many a modern musician cut his teeth on what he picked up through listening to Billy Cotton on a crystal set precariously wired to the bed springs in the school dormitory as an aerial. There was opportunity enough. Billy Cotton was often on the air for an hour and a half at a time. There was one week when he broadcast every night. He was the first band leader who was allowed to announce himself: 'This is Billy Cotton's band playing from Ciro's' – and, being Billy Cotton, he was not always satisfied with an announcement, but slipped in the occasional gag. The BBC seemed to like it.

The broadcasts from Ciro's saw the launching of the song 'Goodnight, Sweetheart', in which Billy had a very influential guiding hand. He always remembered its birth. 'That great song was written by Ray Noble, with whom I always had a wonderful relationship. We recorded for the same company, but on different labels. I suppose I was brassier and more the entertainment type, while he relied on his classy band and his wonderful arrangements. But he was the sort of man who would always pay a joking tribute to me, even in the middle of a performance. If he wrote in a "hot" passage in the middle of an arrangement he would acknowledge "By arrangement with Billy Cotton", or some similar piece of micky-taking.

'One morning I walked into the office of Jimmy Campbell, the song publisher, and found Ray messing about with a small manuscript. "Hello, Bill," he said. "I've been listening to your broadcasts. Very nice indeed. They're not all off the cuff, are they? Where do you get your arrangements?" I told him my pianist Clem Bernard did some. Ray was most interested, and we talked. "I'll tell you what I've got here," he said. "I may sell it to these villains" – indicating Jimmy Campbell – "but I wonder if you'd like to hear it. If it appeals to you, as I think it will, perhaps you'll stick it in on your broadcast from Ciro's tonight."

'I heard the song and I liked it. Jimmy Campbell said, "Try and do it, for my sake." I replied, "Balderdash!" – or words to that effect – "I'm not doing it for you. I like the song, and I like Ray, and we work for the same gramophone company."

'I telephoned Clem Bernard and told him, "I've got something here from Ray Noble, and I think it's very good, and I would like to get it in tonight before Ambrose gets it." Clem came up to my office in Denmark Street and suggested that we could do a small orchestration. So he sat down and rushed out a three-saxophone/trombone and trumpet arrangement. Sid Buckman sang it in the arrangement with the band the same night, and nobody needs reminding what happened to it after that. It soared from the start like a rocket. It has always been a great tune.

'But the point that story makes is the *opportunity* that could be snatched for a writer and his song at that time. This is a typical example of the way in which songs were written and got out. You needed the writer, but you also needed the occasion and the man who had the opportunity to make it go straight away.'

Billy Cotton was now about to emerge as the prince of the show band business. The most famous personality of this period was another prince, the Prince of Wales, later King Edward VIII, who made Ciro's his favourite haunt. The directors of the club appreciated the compliment, but the fame it brought them was not always accompanied by an increase in affluence, since the club was not always the free-spending, rather rollicking (in a refined way) place that it had been before. 'I think,' Billy Cotton hazarded, 'that from the business point of view he went rather too much. The directors would have liked a more free-and-easy atmosphere. But when he came in he put the mockers on, and nobody let their hair down at all. He would come in with the lady he was escorting and with Brigadier Trotter, the equerry who used to go around with him, and by the time all due deference had been paid to him and the wine list was presented there was more than a deathly hush in the club that night.

'I would do my best to tempt people to get up and dance to the liveliest tunes, but I was always brought up short when a request came from H.R.H. to play the "Waltz Intermezzo" from *Cavalleria Rusticana*. Hardly anybody else would dance to it. One night the manager came up with this command for the third time, and I remarked, "Go and ask the silly so-and-so if he knows any other tune." This was not exactly the most tactful comment to make on the heir to the throne, and the next night Lord Tennyson, one of the club committee, saw me early in the evening before the club got lively. "I can't gloss over this," he began. "I like you, Bill, and I like the band, but I think we are due for a change of scene with the Heir knocking around. I know how exasperating a request becomes when it is constantly repeated, and I know that your concern was that people should dress the floor and dance. But he is who he is. It is not done to ask the staff to enquire of the Heir whether the silly so-and-so knows another tune. The next thing will be that you are saying it aloud. I hope you're going to do what I ask. Will you go to Ciro's in Paris and do three months there?"

'I went to Paris, and we had a very successful season there. The Chief of Police liked us so much that he even tried to bring pressure on the French

Musicians' Union to have our stay extended, for they had already invented the gambit whereby they had to pay a French band of the same calibre for doing nothing while *we* played. We certainly pulled in the crowds. You couldn't get in the Paris Ciro's. It was packed solid. I thought to myself, "Why can't we get the Londoners to enjoy themselves like that?"'

When Billy got back to the London Ciro's after his three-month stint in Paris he found a revolution. The band that had followed him in had been Noble Sissle's, the coloured band which had previously been playing at Ciro's in Paris, and the Prince of Wales himself had asked for the substitution. 'Noble Sissle was putting on a wonderful show,' Billy later confessed, 'but the Prince of Wales would never have taken it from me. Formerly they had complained about my band being noisy, but Noble Sissle was making a tremendous sound, trombones blaring, saxes wailing, and he was not only playing for dancing on the floor but had introduced cabaret, step dancing, the lot. One of the directors took me up to the balcony and said, "Well, I suppose you will never forgive us. This is not the same sound that we insisted you should play." But the club was full as well as lively, and I nodded towards the Prince of Wales at his table. "You've got the man in the corner down there, and it's done with his blessing," I replied. When it was my turn to go in again to Ciro's I was permitted to play the same sort of thing.'

Jimmy Phillips, the music publisher who was a lifelong friend of Bill Cotton's, remembers that when Bill *did* have words to say to the Prince of Wales he was not as tactless as the club director, Lord Tennyson, apparently feared. 'The Prince of Wales used to get up and play the drums in the band,' says Jimmy, 'but Bill did not like it, and said so. The management would say to Bill, "Don't refuse him, Bill, don't cross him. Let him do whatever he wants, he is the Prince of Wales." But Bill got his way and they told the Prince of Wales that he could not get up and play the drums any more in Billy Cotton's band. Bill won the day, but he had a way of getting on with very high-class people.'

Bill did indeed have a way of getting on with them – and sometimes very much to his own advantage. 'Things sometimes used to liven up when the men had had a drink or two,' he used to recount. 'They had an itch for trying to conduct the band. "I'll conduct now, Cotton," somebody like Lord Northesk would say, and I would answer, "It will cost you a bottle of Scotch." They used to send a bottle to the band room, and I had more Scotch there in the end than they had in the bar. I added to my cellar by winning shooting matches. Ferrari, the head waiter, let me put a twenty-five-yard target down in the Grill, and I used to take the members on for a bottle

Billy Cotton with some of the band.

of Scotch. Some of them were too far under the weather even to see the target.'

Jimmy Phillips has an amusing anecdote about Bill's dress clothes: 'When he was musical director for the General Theatre Corporation he had a very smart dinner jacket, splits at the back, crafty pockets and all that jazz. When he knew he was going into Ciro's I said to him, "You will have to get a proper suit for there. You have to look right: a bit of class, full dress, tails, you know." So I took him to Tepesch, the tailor who made suits for the band, and said, "Can you do something quickly?" Tepesch made a tail suit in two days, and Bill went round and collected it and brought it to my office. "What a load of crap!" was his opinion. I said, "What do you mean? It's great. It's beautiful!" Bill said, "Get away, don't be silly, I look like a poof in it." I said, "You look fantastic." He gave me such a bad time about it that I was embarrassed, because he had paid a fortune for it. Anyway, he walked into Ciro's that night, and Louis, the maître d'hôtel, walked up and exclaimed, "Bill, what a marvellous suit! Congratulations!" Then, after that, Bill went mad about the suit.'

BILLY STARTS THE BAND SHOW BOOM

Jimmy Phillips was the one who had 'chatted' Bill into applying for an audition at Ciro's in the first place, and both were naturally delighted when he got the job. According to Jimmy, 'Bill had a great time at Ciro's. It was, of course, a hell of a jump from the Astoria.' When he relieved Noble Sissle, after the spell in Paris, Bill wooed back into his band the famous coloured dancer and trombone player Ellis Jackson, who had teamed up with Noble Sissle. 'I had met him when I was at Wembley in 1924,' Bill recalled, 'and now I took him for my next venture, which was the sheer entertainment and show band exploitation that I had always been working towards.'

This next venture, the first regular Band Show, which Billy had been shaping since his experimentation at Southport, came about through what seemed at first to be a spell of bad luck. After a notable run at Ciro's Bill was laid low by an incapacitating illness, and it was while he was pulling himself together again that the opportunity occurred. 'In 1931 an agent called Michel told me he wanted to put my band in at the Alhambra, Leicester Square, as the second half of a cinema show. I was very anxiously collecting a band together again, for I had just had a bout of rheumatic fever which crossed me off the active list, and several of the members of my band had left. The most notable loss was the disappearance of my brass section. Nat Gonella, Joe Ferrie, and Sid Buckman all joined Roy Fox, who had

A still from one of Billy Cotton's films, *Music Hall Parade*.

just come over from America for the first time. I can't deny that there was a certain tension about this move, but at the time I had no work to offer them, and musicians must live. Nat Gonella came back to me for a spell afterwards.

'The man who came to my rescue was my nephew Laurie Johnson, with whom I had teamed up at the start of my musical career and who had led the band at Wembley. Laurie had been running his own band, and in fact he followed me into the Streatham Locarno and the Rialto, Liverpool. When I was absolutely strapped for want of players after my illness, he just said quietly, "Take any of my men you want." "Well, I'll take you for a start," I said as a joke, and to my amazement he nodded and said, "O.K." Laurie folded up his band, came into mine on fiddle and banjo, and gave me the pick of his men. He always stayed with me after that, so, even allowing for the six-year gap when he was on his own, he became "My old Dutch" and we were able to sing, "We've been together now for forty years."'

Bill always had a reputation in show business for keeping his band together, and he now built up the nucleus of the show band which became such a feature of the great variety days of the 1930s. Clem Bernard stayed on throughout his lifetime as the lively heart of the band. Joe White, on double bass, joined in 1929. Arthur Baker, on drums, came in with Laurie Johnson and Ellis Jackson in 1930. Phil Phillips, on fiddle, joined in 1931. Among the saxes, Mick Burberry, baritone, entered the band in 1930, and Frankie Kenyon and Edgar Bracewell, altos, in 1932.

ENTER ALAN BREEZE

Another member of the show who joined the band in 1932 was Alan Breeze. Here is Breezy's own lively account of how this came about.

'My father, Louis Breeze, was a member of the original D'Oyly Carte Opera Company and later a singing teacher. I started singing as a boy soprano at the age of eleven, and I broadcast from the old 2LO station at Savoy Hill. When my voice broke I had to start all over again, and I began a career in oratorio and concert party work. Early in 1932 I had a few days' work in a film called *The First Mrs Fraser* at Wembley Studios.

'There was a night club sequence in the film in which Bill's band was appearing as the club orchestra, and I, with two or three other singers, had been booked to do the "dubbing" for some of the actors, who evidently hadn't any singing voices. (They were more particular then: if anybody sang he had to have a voice!)

'At that period Bill was concentrating on doing a stage show on the music

31

halls and in the super-cinemas. They used to have two feature films and a stage show. Bill's resident vocalist was a sax player who was very good for dance halls, where in those days they used a megaphone (mikes hadn't yet come into being). But a megaphone didn't look so good on the stage.

'Bill heard me singing in this film. In those days I was more of a straight singer, and I had a very powerful voice. Bill had in his new stage show a concert arrangement of "Trees", and he needed a heavy voice to get above the heavy orchestration. He sent his manager, Dave Toff (now director of his own music publishing company), to find the owner of the voice he had heard, and ask if I'd do an audition. So I went along to the old Hammersmith Palais where Bill was appearing between films, and I took along the number "That's Why Darkies Were Born".

'I gave the audition in Bill's dressing room, which was very small. Clem Bernard brought in his accordion to accompany me, and when I hit the top note old Bill said, "Gawd, that's enough!" I think I nearly deafened him. Then he said, "Yes, that's what I want, son, but can you sing in tempo, you know, keeping strict time?" [It should be explained that Breezy sometimes stutters when he's not singing.] So I drew myself up, all eight and a half stone of me, and I said, "Of c-c-c-course I bleedin' well can, wot d-d-d'yer th-think I've c-c-c-come 'ere f-for?"

'I'll never forget the dumbstruck expression on Bill's face, because in those days he was a very strict disciplinarian, and nobody spoke to him like that. Anyway, Dave Toff came in, and Bill said, "What about six pounds a week for a month's trial?" And I, as casually as I could, without wishing to appear as though Heaven had smiled on me, said, "O.K." Dave typed out the contract on an odd piece of paper, for a month's trial at an all-in salary of six pounds a week. This is the only contract Bill and I ever had between us. I heard later that after I'd gone, Bill said, "Blimey, 'e's a funny bloke, ain't 'e? Cheeky so-and-so an' all, ain't 'e?"

'In the pre-war band there was a marvellous spirit in the outfit. We were more like a big family – very seldom was there any quarrel or bad feeling. We mostly knew each other's little problems and stuck by one another. Naturally we had our little moans, but no worse than in any other closely knit fraternity.

'We were always playing practical jokes on each other, and Bill himself was as bad (or as good) as any of us. A favourite gag happened at the Brixton Astoria. I was in a dressing room on the third floor directly over the stage door, and if Bill or any of the boys were standing outside talking, I used to dash upstairs, fill a paper bag with water, lean out, and drop it on Bill's

Alan Breeze, who joined the band in 1932.

head or on any of the boys who were there. For a while they couldn't find out who was doing it. Then one day I leaned out, and was just about to drop my "bomb" when CRASH – and I was drenched. Apparently Bill had tumbled to who it was, and climbed to the roof above me with a jug of water, waited until I leaned out, and dropped the lot on me.

'Once in the thirties I'd got a sports car of which I was very proud. (Cars were my hobby.) In between shows I'd spend the time cleaning and polishing it. Once I had just stood back to admire my work when PLONK – a paper bag of water landed on the bonnet, all beautifully polished as it had been, from the roof of the Finsbury Park Astoria.

'Then I remember we were once doing a number called "Any Rags, Bottles or Bones" – a rather sad number in which I did a monologue about my little wife, Jenny, who'd died, and I still carried on alone. I used to sing, from the wings, "Any rags, bottles or bones" and then pick up a sack and walk on carrying it, singing the number. The sack was usually filled with paper and rags. This time, I left it till the last minute to pick it up. To my horror, I could hardly lift it. The boys had put two or three counterweights in it, twenty-eight pounds each. I wasn't very strong, but I staggered on with it and had to hold it all through the number – I dared not put it down, because it would have made a crash, and I doubt if I could have lifted it up again.

'We often did a choral number in the show, and we'd all go out front with a spot on us, and the stage blacked out. Bill would creep along and put drawing pins on some of our seats. So when we dashed back and sat down, and then stood to take a bow, you can imagine us trying to hide our sudden stab of pain. Lots of gags like this used to happen, no harm and nothing vicious in them. We were an all-male band in those days. The only time Bill had a girl singer was as a guest on a broadcast or recording session, or some occasion like that.

'I started singing comedy numbers by accident. Bill used to have a comedy singer called Fred Douglas on his recording sessions. At one session he was ill and couldn't turn up. Bill had a comedy record to make, and of course he was stuck – it was a number that needed some different dialects. I said, "I'll have a go at it." Bill said, "What, you? You can't do it, you're a bleedin' opera singer." Anyway, in the end he let me have a go, and much to his astonishment it came off. He said, "Why didn't you tell me you could do all this?" I replied, "Well, you never asked, did you?"

'Then we started putting more individual comedy and light numbers in the stage show, which meant I was in practically every number in our stage

34

act, except for Ellis Jackson's dance number. (Ellis is one of the most remarkable men I've ever met, and I think the fittest; he must be nearer ninety than eighty years old now, and is still doing his early morning run, plus exercise, and an occasional show. His number was always one of the biggest hits of our stage act.)

'Naturally, therefore, I was working extremely hard, working out front in most numbers, five shows a day, and often in those days an hour-and-a-half broadcast from 10.30 to midnight in which I was the only singer. (Mum used to keep a list, and in several of these broadcasts I sang twenty-six to twenty-eight numbers.)

'Then Bill got another tenor sax in, who doubled as a vocalist – Chips Chippendale – and he was able to help me out a lot. Then, in about 1936 I think, Chips left us and we got a very good straight tenor vocalist, Peter Williams. We used to put a straight ballad in the show then, like "Smilin' Through" or "Sylvia", and we put back a strictly straight version of "Trees". Peter was and is a very nice bloke and was very popular, but he left us early in the war and went into Bristol Aircraft.

'Earlier we also had Teddy Foster in the band, and he used to do a spot in our stage act, an impression of Louis Armstrong which he put over marvellously – and this also gave me a rest. Jack Doyle joined us, also working in the Armstrong style, but he was a very good eccentric dancer and used to interpolate this in his spot.

'Clem Bernard, our pianist and arranger, was the mainstay of the band – a really lovely man and a very dear friend of Rene [Alan's wife] and me. In fact, he used to live with us most of the time during and after the war, because his home was in Southport. His death was a terrible loss to us all and it hit me extremely hard. Rene says I've never been the same since we lost him. He and I had the same sense of humour, and we used to work out most of the comedy numbers between us.

'To sum up Bill: I found him a strict man, a disciplinarian, a tough man outwardly; but a natural man, who hated snobbery and couldn't stand shallowness and artificiality and wasn't afraid to say so – a trait which, I fear, made him some enemies. He was a good, perhaps over-cautious businessman. He was a man with the gift of a very musical ear, and with the flair for knowing the type of number or show that appealed to "ordinary people" – often to the frustration of musicians and some of our arrangers. He had no time for anything "twee" or "arty". I've known him cut what was to us a beautiful part, or chorus, in an arrangement and give voice to his favourite phrase in justification: "No. The station master at Wigan wouldn't

35

like that." I remember in the early days, the late Peter Yorke brought up an arrangement of "The Moon Is Yellow" for me to sing at the Dominion, Tottenham Court Road. It was musically a very beautiful orchestration, and Bill cut about a third of it. Poor old Peter was heart-broken, and said afterwards, "The man's not a musician, he's a bloody butcher!"

'But Bill did a lot of very good things that he didn't talk about: like sending an allowance to the mother of one of our original guitarists who died; seeing to the education of the son of our old drummer who was killed in action just at the end of the war; and I think he used to send an allowance to Clem's wife. These things he never spoke about, and if they did get mentioned, or if he was asked about them, he would be most embarrassed.

'Yes, in my eyes Bill Cotton was a great bloke, and I had the deepest admiration for him – his toughness, his determination, and, most of all, underneath everything, his kindness and softness. I used to call him "the poor man's Churchill". In fact, in one of our stage shows he used to give an impression of him. I'd copy Churchill's voice and Bill would mime it, because he had a great physical resemblance to Churchill.'

BUILDING THE BAND

Everyone's memories of Bill Cotton reflect the same warmth as Breezy's. And because of Bill's knack for keeping a band together as friends, this warmth became part of their professional aura. But in the beginning, Bill was very tentatively feeling his way. 'We went to the Alhambra as pioneers for a trial month. I was really very green as a show-band leader, with little idea of what the public wanted. The number that saved my bacon was "All the King's Horses", and I think the reason why that was such a success was that I had had the sense to buy some sleigh-bells and make something of a novelty number of it. The people loved it, though I confess that at the time I thought it was pretty terrible. It certainly began to change my ideas as to what was demanded as all-round entertainment, and probably began to mould my image – which I was later to admit to unashamedly – as a "round gent making a square sound".'

The Alhambra season was the start of the great boom in ciné-variety. Very soon the idea was taken up by the Paramount circuit, and they signed Billy up. In one month he would cover four Paramount theatres in London – the Dominion, halls at Streatham and Brixton, and any London super-cinema that could grab him. Then he would go out to the provinces – to Birmingham, Leeds, Manchester, Sheffield, Liverpool, Newcastle, and all over the place. It was at about this time that he introduced as his signature

The start of 'When Cotton Papered the Office',
a 'Cotton Caper' from the Billy Cotton Band
Show series of 1963.

Kathie Kay, Alan Breeze, and the Silhouettes in
'Any Old Iron', a finale from the 1963 series of
shows.

tune 'Somebody Stole My Gal'. There was no particular significance about it. Laurie Johnson explained it by alleging, 'Bill is always stealing somebody's girl, anyway.' But Bill saw it merely as a good bouncy tune which was characteristic of the sort of show he was offering.

Bill himself was blossoming in stagecraft. He had his unerring ear for popular music. He had his very sound business sense. But he also had a sense of responsibility for the 'boys' whom he had signed on in his band. Their livelihood, as he understood it, was in his hands. Just as he never wanted to let the public down, he never wanted to let his boys down. He therefore consciously sought to form a policy for his band show. He realized that there was a lot to learn. 'I knew that everything depended on my own efforts. I began to develop as an entertainer. I knew it was a new business, and I never kidded myself that I understood it by any form of instinct. I realized I knew precious little about it. I made up my mind that, as I started touring, it was going to be a long and rocky road. I had no tradition behind me. The business I was doing, which was giving British variety a shot in the arm, was something that had to be learned and mastered.

'And so I formed my own ambitions for show business. I adopted a saying: "I don't want to teach anybody anything." I wanted to play what people liked and what they clapped. In spite of my long interest in what had been considered the advanced American music, I made up my mind not to be a pioneer. I was concerned with good dancing music in a dance hall and good show band stuff in a theatre. I had a band to support and a bank balance to keep up in order to support those boys. So I kept off the pioneering in my gramophone work, too. The sort of discs I made were the sort of discs which experienced men in the industry were pretty sure would go over big. A typical example is "In Eleven More Months and Ten More Days I'll Be Out of the Calaboose". I didn't agree with this at first. I was more attracted to something slightly phrased and hot, like "Bessie Couldn't Help It". I protested to my A & R man when he picked "Eleven More Months", but he said, "Bill, you're a fool if you don't play it." And he was right. It sold like hot cakes. And I suppose the justification of his stand against mine is that Jimmy Grafton was putting that tune into the television Band Show comedy numbers thirty years later. I never knew him work in "Bessie Couldn't Help It".'

As a band-leader on the music hall stage, Billy Cotton kept his eyes and ears very keenly open to acquire as much experience as he possibly could. 'Striving to make myself more professional as an entertainer, I had the enormous advantage of playing in the same theatres as the real professionals. I

Billy Cotton once literally brought the house
down. Fortunately it was during rehearsal and
no one was hurt. Strangely enough, one of the
effects in the script that day was 'Noise of
studio falling in'.

Bill in the cockpit of his Gipsy Moth at
Croydon.

observed very closely performers like Will Hay, whose personal genius, as well as timing and presentation, taught me so much. They were real masters. They didn't need spotlights to pick them out. Their personalities lit up the stage. They had the sense of timing to short-cut their comedy. Will Hay had his schoolmaster act in which one of the boys stood up with his hand up. Will Hay didn't waste time by asking, "What do you want?" Everybody knew what the boy wanted. All Will Hay said was "No!" as soon as the boy put his hand up. I learned not to explain a joke if it is a good one, not to spoil it by over-dressing.'

As the great band show boom of the thirties got under way, Billy Cotton and his band were signed up in the memorable series of Blue Star Flying Visits to the various Mecca dance halls which were being established all over the country. Bill took the job so seriously that he literally flew to many of the bookings. He bought a Moth aircraft with a Gipsy III engine and, with Laurie Johnson 'riding pillion', went by air to any engagement where there was a convenient airfield. 'Flying that Gipsy Moth was a fulfilment in itself,' he confessed. 'Nothing gave me more pleasure than to go down to Croydon before the sun rose, wheel the aeroplane out of the hangar, turn the prop myself, kick away the chocks, hop aboard, and soar up into the dark sky just before the dawn. I would climb to around six thousand feet and watch the sun come up. I could see it alone, for myself, before the people who were earthbound below. It was perfect up there, beautiful, restful, an escape, an adventure. Flying was my indulgence and my compensation.'

He also compensated himself for his restless career round the music halls of Britain with motor-racing. He had raced on sand at Southport, but his habit of flying from Brooklands Flying Club (now the great BAC complex near Weybridge) inevitably introduced him to the Brooklands Racing Circuit. In 1935 he tuned up a Riley Nine and nonchalantly entered it for the British Racing Drivers' five-hundred-mile race. The engine blew up after twenty-two minutes. Next year he drove his MG K3 Magnette in the Long Handicap and finished in second place. The race was held at Whitsun, and he had beaten (a handicapped) Earl Howe in a 3·3 GP Bugatti. On the autumn bank holiday of the same year Bill won the Long Handicap at 106·94 miles an hour. The following month he entered the BRDC five-hundred-mile, in which he had blown up the previous year, and the British Empire Trophy, coming fifth and third respectively. He was elected to the British Racing Drivers' Club, and went up to Southport to drive Sir Malcolm Campbell's first Sunbeam *Bluebird* at 121·57 m.p.h. over the flying kilometre. Next year he won the Easter Short Handicap at Brooklands, doing

Billy Cotton winning the Southport 100-Mile
Race in 1937, from *The Motor*.

The Duke of Kent wishes the Great Britain
team well before the British Grand Prix of
1938.

a flying lap at 113·19 m.p.h. Switching between the MG and an ERA that year, he won races at Dublin and Southport, and did 123·89 m.p.h. at Brooklands, being one of only five MG drivers in the history of the course to gain the 120 m.p.h. badge. In 1938 he represented Great Britain in the Grand Prix at Donington, driving $1\frac{1}{2}$-litre ERAs against 3-litre Mercedes-Benzes being driven for Germany. Nuvolari took the individual title in an Auto-Union, and the ERAs won the team prize, after warm wishes personally delivered by the Duke of Kent (a photograph of which delivery Billy never tired of turning up).

The Band Show went on. During the years leading up to World War II, Billy Cotton was a very determined business man in show business, candidly having his sport as an indulgence, but only when it did not harm the band, and then taking every chance to play as hard as he had worked. He saw his band as a unit, not as a cradle for the star system. 'I decided that teamwork was going to be my policy,' he said. 'I have found many good men for key positions in my band, but they stayed *in* my band, not in front of it. Besides instrumental virtuosity the one quality I sought and developed in my boys was an *esprit de corps*.'

BILLY LAYS IT ON THE LINE

Billy Cotton committed himself to a remarkable statement of the principles by which he intended to run his band. It is as shrewd as it is honest, and the very first sentence gives Bill's own side of the confrontation with devoted artistic arrangers mentioned earlier in connection with poor Peter Yorke. 'Special material,' decreed Bill, 'has to be used with the utmost discretion. When musicians goggle at a new arrangement and declare it marvellous, my tendency is to reach for my pruning-knife. The public likes nothing that it can't understand. No hot solo goes in unless it sets my own feet tapping. I see myself as a typical member of my audience.'

And so the show still went on! And then, in the middle of the laughter, and the hard work, and the harder play that Bill was giving himself on the race-track and in the air, everybody suddenly found that the thirties had finished and the Second World War had begun.

THE BAND IN WAR-TIME

On 3 September 1939 Pilot Officer Cotton was already enrolled in the Reserve of Royal Air Force officers, and he reported immediately to Uxbridge. After an exhaustive medical examination he went before a board presided over by Air Marshal Gossage, who said to him, 'I really must congratulate you. According to your medical examination you are one of the fittest persons of your age we have ever met. Now, what do you think you can do?'

'I think I could be useful for ditch-flying,' said Bill, and he got the impression that the board agreed. He was referring to air-sea rescue by aircraft, not by motor launches, because he was already accustomed to landing in the sea thanks to his anti-submarine course in the previous war. But the outcome was different – though perhaps mercifully different – as Bill later jauntily recounted.

'I had a friend, Windsor Richards, a man I used to race with, who had put in for the same work. We waited to be posted for training on the Walrus seaplanes that were then to be used for landing in the sea and picking up pilots who had had to ditch. Richards got his posting quickly – and almost his first action was to come down into the sea to rescue a German pilot. The pilot of another Me 109 shot him up and killed him.

'But when my posting came along it shook me. I was to report to Northolt to proceed as adjutant to a mobile squadron. Adjutant! An admin job! Cotton, the king of the office! I thought I'd be a notable failure there. So I asked for another interview with Air Marshal Gossage. He said, "You know there's a war on. There can be no picking and choosing." "I'm only picking and choosing for the sake of old England," I assured him. "The country doesn't know what threatens it if you put me in an office. I can't even write properly, sir. It has got worse recently. I don't think I can write at all. Even on my cheques I have to sign with a cross. In any case, I have a pilot's licence. I am only forty, and I should find it easy to take a conversion course to Walruses, because I already have experience of landing on floats in a DH6 from the last war." The air marshal pointed out that according to my records I had a defect in my left eye. This had been a boob on my part at the medical board. I had forgotten to follow my usual drill in these affairs and learn the optical chart by heart for the first four lines. "LPRFDZ" – I used to be able to reel them off as some people can memorize a typewriter keyboard. But it was difficult enough to disguise this particular disability. All my publicity photographs had shown me wearing spectacles for donkey's years. It had not affected my ability to fly solo, however, or to win races at Brooklands, and I reminded him of this.

'The air marshal thought for a moment. He was smiling a bit, and I thought he might ask for one of my cheques as a souvenir. "Do you know, Cotton, what you would be good for?" he said. "Why don't you ask ENSA to request us to loan you to them, and then we will attach you to Air Force

44

service, and we will send you with your band to entertain our men in France. But you must, of course, entertain as many of the Army as can get in to your concerts."

'Active service! I thought. Why can't they let me be a hero? Then I thought of all those rubber stamps they were planning for me to take charge of in an adjutant's office. "If that suits you, sir, it will suit me," I told the air marshal, and I went back to London. I re-organized the band, and we went off to France to entertain the squadrons through the first winter of the war. It was winter, all right, the coldest ever, as every man who was out there will remember.

'We used to go to our assignments by motor-coach. One night we were to play at Lens, a sizeable industrial centre in northern France amongst the First World War battlefields. The troops were to come in from surrounding camps. Somewhere near Bar-le-Duc our coach was directed across a newly erected army bridge, but it proved too heavy for the construction the engineers had put up. We were sinking into the water when we dived out of the coach just in time. We got to the right side of the stream and waited for fresh transport to be sent to take us on our way. We hadn't too far to go. While we were waiting we went into a local café near a British aerodrome. There was a sign up saying "Bacon and Eggs", and a smell that advertised the product far better than the sign. We had had nothing but tinned bacon on rations, which never fried into anything but a gloppy fat goo, and we had never known of a French café that served bacon at all. So we scrambled for it at speed. There were a number of off-duty British pilots who were obviously savouring the luck of having this unusual pub as their local, and the meal we had certainly lived up to its promise, marvellous bacon and eggs à l'anglaise.

'We went on our way rejoicing and finally arrived at Lens. Two thousand soldiers and airmen were coming in from camps all round. The weather was the usual bitter cold, and there was ice on the hats of the men as they got down from their trucks. The shed we played in was so cold that they had to pass a mug of hot rum grog along the front row of my band so that their hot alcoholic breath would melt the frozen pads on their instruments. We played the tunes of the moment: the quick ones that had been written the week the war broke out, like "We're Gonna Hang Out the Washing on the Siegfried Line", which, I hope, the fellows regarded with the necessary cynicism; the sentimental ones, which I hope they liked better, like "Wish Me Luck as You Wave Me Goodbye"; and the classics of the war which really had nothing to do with the war at all,-like "South of the

45

Border". I think it was a reasonably good show, and the boys enjoyed it.

'The coach called for my band afterwards, but an English brigadier in local command, who had enjoyed the concert, quickly fixed up an impromptu party and asked me to stay. There was a lot of talk during the course of the night about my motor-racing at Brooklands and the other tracks during the previous years, and when the brigadier took me home in his big Service Humber perhaps he thought he was on his mettle. "If I can say one thing," I told him, "be careful with your foot on the brake, for the road is like glass." There was a sheet of ice over everything. We got up the hill to Vimy Ridge, and there was a long avenue of trees going down. He went careering down it, came to a bend, touched the brakes, and wrapped us round a tree. I put my knees against the dashboard in self-protection, and got them severely bruised. The brigadier went straight through the windscreen and had his face badly cut.

'We pulled ourselves together and staggered and limped, streaming with blood, the three kilometres to Arras. It was three o'clock in the morning. I rang the night bell of the Hôtel Crillon, where I was staying, and the owner, Madame Rapoche, who usually waited up for me, appeared in the doorway. She took one look at us, spattered with blood and freezing to death, but not even that sight could shake off her usual reprimand. "You naughty boy!" she said. "Where have you been? You're late again."

'Two days later I was telling the tale of this eventful evening in idle talk at the bar of the Lion d'Or in Reims. An intelligence officer, Flight Lieutenant Henry Merckel, did not seem at all interested in our dicing with death, but seemed remarkably interested in my account of the café by the aerodrome. "A Frenchman who cooks bacon and eggs?" he queried. "That's rather remarkable. Where did you say it was?" We told him. Next time I saw him in the Lion d'Or he said, "Your chap up at Bar-le-Duc won't be cooking any more bacon and eggs for a spell." I asked him what he meant. "He was found to be a member of the fifth column," Merckel explained. "We searched his café and found a radio transmitter. His speciality of bacon and eggs was a lure to get the RAF boys in, and even from the guarded private chatter of the men off duty he got a valuable hint or two about operations either planned or cancelled. He passed it on by radio to the Germans."'

All through that winter Billy Cotton and his band got on with their job. 'Looking back,' he said later, 'I'm glad of what work we could do. It doesn't matter what particular tunes we played then, or the jokes we made or the songs we sang. All I remember is the atmosphere we made between us, a parcel of boys in a band and sometimes a sparse RAF detachment, sometimes company after company of soldiers trucking in from their billets – far from home, a home which many of them were never to see again, for Dunkirk lay ahead.'

When the German breakthrough came, the band was sent home. Billy continued in charge of Air Training Corps entertainment. He was attached to the Windsor Squadron, but he had an Air Ministry pass entitling him to get help from any aerodrome to promote any entertainment, and this permit took him to every town where there was an air training squadron. He still toured with the band, but he put the Royal Air Force first. And his pride was overflowing when his elder son, Ted, became a Mosquito pilot.

At about this time Bill became acquainted with Lew and Leslie Grade, and Leslie became his agent. According to Bill, 'There are many stories I could tell of the times he and I had together with his brother Lew. I believe Lew's favourite story concerns a period when I was always wanting to work in London, and one day they told me that there just weren't any more theatres left for me to play. I immediately hit the roof and said I was packing it all in. "You'll be back!" shouted Lew, as I stormed out of the door. Sure enough, I was – I'd left my hat behind. Soon after I joined him Leslie went into the Royal Air Force. I remember well that wherever he was stationed they used to get better concerts than the shows currently running at the Palladium.'

Leslie Grade is much more explicit about Bill's attachment to London. 'I met Bill through arranging an engagement for him at the Stoll Theatre, Kingsway. We became very close. I was in the Air Force, at that moment stationed at Hendon. Our friendship deepened, and he told me he was particularly anxious to play engagements in London. He did not want to go out of London with his band if he could help it. This was very surprising, as most other star performers wanted to play outside London, because of the Blitz. But Billy used to drive me crazy saying that he must play in London. I used to say to him, "Shall we get some new theatres built in London?"

'He then asked me to become his agent, and I was delighted to do so. This was a big thing for me, because he was a very important star and an extremely nice person. I represented him for many years, together, of course, with my brother, now Lord Grade. We worked very closely together, in the Lew and Leslie Grade Agency which is now the Grade Organisation. I remember that Bill's show was always very good indeed, and he was always meticulous about the type of show he did. He would not have any dirt. In my opinion the show was the best that any British band has ever put on. It was very funny, and great entertainment. The arrangement I usually

47

had with him was that we would present the show at each theatre together, and after he received his salary and the band their salary and all the artists on the show were paid, we would share any profits left over. Bill was very generous in that way. When he became a bigger star than ever through his Sunday radio show he insisted on never altering these arrangements. We carried on for years very successfully. We were close personal friends, besides our business relationship, and I often used to go to his home in Farnham Common for Sunday lunch. When he used to drive me back to London he always used to say to me, "Have you ever been in a car at a hundred miles an hour?" And through those back country roads into London he used to drive at a hundred miles an hour and frighten me to death. He was a great friend to me in every possible way. As a matter of fact, when I returned to London from my overseas service I even bought his house at Farnham Common, as he wanted to move elsewhere.

'He was a great star. I shall never forget all the wonderful times we had together. He made people happy, which I know was what he wanted. Wherever he and his band appeared they were a tremendous attraction, and it is very hard to find attractions of that nature today. In my opinion his was the only band show that really meant anything on a variety stage. Of course, there are many big bands today that do business in dance halls and Sunday concerts and things like that, but I don't think there is any band in this country today that could stand up to Billy Cotton and his Band as an entertainment and as a box office attraction in the theatres. Whenever he went to a theatre you always knew you were going to have a good week's business. Everybody liked him, from the poorest to the richest.

'He was always very sensitive, always very concerned if anything in his show upset anyone. He was really upset after one of his regular Sunday broadcasts when a man telephoned him at the studio and told him he was very offended by one of the songs he had done. It was called "I Went to a Wedding" and it was about a Jewish wedding. This upset Bill tremendously. He called me immediately afterwards and asked me if I thought the song was offensive. I said I did not think it was offensive in any way at all, and if he cut it out of his programme I myself would be very upset, because it was a very nice sort of comedy song. But this worrying about whether he had done right or not just shows the type of man he was.'

Opposite Bill's war-time home at Farnham Common lived his friend Jimmy Phillips, the music publisher. 'Sometimes,' Bill later reminisced, 'I would come back from work at midnight and keep him company in the air raid warden post he ran. We used to get a bit of fun even out of that.

Leslie Grade, Bill's agent for many years.

I was mucking about with ladders and buckets in the post one night when a clergyman came in. He introduced himself with what I thought was a little too much pomp, which some men derive from the pulpit. "I am the Reverend So-and-so," he announced, "and I have been told by the General" – who was in charge of all defence in Buckinghamshire – "to report to the man in charge. Are you in charge?" he asked me.

'I was just doing a bit of voluntary labour, looking like Rob Wilton in a steel helmet. But I was senior man at the post at the time, and I told him so. He decided to examine us on our capability. He took up a sheet of incident papers. "Now," he said, "in the case of an incident during the night, what does one do with this?" I looked at the paper in his hand, and then I looked meaningfully at the rest of the men in the post. "If any of you beggars tells him what to do with that paper," I warned, "I'll kill him." So the reverend reported me to the general, but there was no chain of command that could catch me.'

When the Blitz eased off London, Billy Cotton consented to go out into the provinces again – but, of course, the Blitz had moved there, too. It really seemed as if he was chasing the bombardment. Not that he didn't take evasive action when necessary. 'I was having supper in the Adelphi Hotel at Liverpool, when they dropped a bomb just by me. For the rest of the week I spent the night going backwards and forwards on the all-night ferry across the Mersey (the captain let me kip there), on the reasoning that if you couldn't escape a direct hit, at least the misses wouldn't rock you so much. I had an engagement in Plymouth, and when I was chatting in the bar before the show someone boasted that they had the situation absolutely under control, declaring that they had more guns in Plymouth than Hitler had aircraft in the sky. I said, "Don't say that, whatever you do, because you are just asking for it." I was a bit superstitious about touching wood, you see. Just at that moment two air raid wardens staggered in with their faces terribly burned. I think they had been caught by flares that the bombers used to drop before a raid, or a few gas incendiaries. Then the real bombardment started. That night the stage where we were appearing had a direct hit and was wiped out completely. And the Royal Hotel, where I was staying, went up in flames. Laurie Johnson and I got as many of the boys as possible into our cars and we went out onto the moors until six in the morning. Then we came back to start clearing up.'

BILL HERBERT

During the Battle of Britain there had been a mortal blight on all show busi-

50

ness, and many performers went into war industry, among them Bill Herbert. 'I had been conducting the Billy Cotton Band Round-Up Show on tour, when the war got serious and everything stopped. I got a job in a factory machine shop making shock absorbers for tanks, because I had a certain amount of technical ability.'

One Saturday afternoon he had a couple of hours off and went for a stroll through Shepherds Bush. The Billy Cotton Band happened to be playing at the Empire, so Bill Herbert decided to wait at the stage door to catch some of his friends after the show. When Billy Cotton saw him he asked Bill if he could go down to Bristol the next week to do a broadcast with the band as they needed a guitar player.

As Bill Herbert recalls, 'I had a drink with the lads, and I went back to Bill and I said, "Well, I'll try this. Yes, I'll come." So Bill said to Fred, his stage manager, "Give him a railway ticket to Bristol for Sunday." I had to go into the factory on Sunday up till dinner-time, so I went in on Sunday morning and cleared everything up, all the work I had, and got everything set and came out and got on the train for Bristol. I did a week's broadcasting with them. Then I went back the following week to the factory. They thought I'd been off ill. I never said anything.

'Two or three weeks later the band were in London and Bill asked me to work with him for the week. I could work that in a bit more easily. I spent the afternoons broadcasting and the early evenings on stage, and I worked in the factory round the rest of the day. On the Saturday night we went round to the pub for a drink after the show, and he said, "Could you join me permanently? I'm starting a run at Watford on Monday and I must have a guitar player. And you've got the stage experience I want." I decided to go in with him, and on the Sunday morning I went in and cleared my tools up and walked out. And on the Monday I started with him and I stayed with him for the rest of the band's time – some twenty-eight years, for I started at the very end of 1941.

'I did all the tours with him, and was involved in the comedy numbers. I was very useful to him because I could arrange music.'

THE REMARKABLE ELLIS JACKSON

Billy Cotton had his own memories of Bill Herbert's arrangements, and as usual they contained a candid admission that his own judgement was sometimes wrong. 'I was always conservative. I never welcomed changes, and took some time to admit that I liked them even when I did. I remember I once asked Bill Herbert if he ought not to do something about another

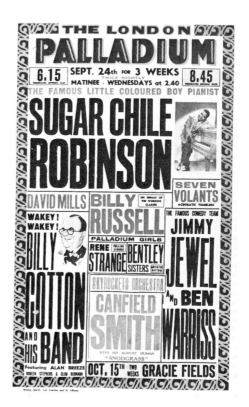

arrangement for Ellis Jackson's spot – he had really been doing his medley of Strauss numbers for too many years. Bill said he would knock together a medley of old Southern tunes, and he spent six weeks collecting them, knitting them together, compiling the score, and rehearsing around the piano. We had a last full rehearsal all Saturday afternoon at the Croydon Empire, intending to try it out in the show the following Monday. I said afterwards to Bill, "If I was paying my half-crown to see this show, I wouldn't go a lot on this thing you've done for Jackson." "Don't you like it?" he asked. "Well, I don't know." "Don't you want to try it?" "Oh, try it out, try it out, but you'll be hearing from me if I don't like it."

'As it happened, at the second house that Saturday night Ellis Jackson pulled a muscle in his leg and couldn't dance for a fortnight; he had to stick to playing the trombone. We finally put his act in at the Shepherds Bush Empire after rehearsing it on the Monday afternoon. Just before the spot was due I saw Jackson look across to Herbert as if to say, "This is it." And Bill Herbert put his thumb up. I announced Jackson, and he did his act, and he hit them like a bomb. In the middle of the storming applause I said to Herbert, "Well, I suppose I was wrong!" So the next time, I let Jackson's act go only two years before I changed it. Bill Herbert put together the *Yankee Doodle Dandy* tunes into a dance routine. We put that on first at the London Palladium on a Tuesday opening night. I have never heard such applause. Jackson took umpteen curtain calls, and the papers were full of "the little coloured man who stopped the show at the Palladium".

'Ellis Jackson is a remarkable man. I first met him the year I started my professional career. He was working in a club called Moody's in the Tottenham Court Road, and I used to drop in there with Laurie Johnson when we had the band at Wembley in 1924. The drinking laws were very tight then, and Jackson used to complain that whenever I went into the club it was raided. He was in Noble Sissle's band that followed me into Ciro's from Paris, and I nabbed him when I started touring. And he was with me on my last touring engagement when I played the club at Batley. He still works the clubs, playing trombone, telling stories, dancing. He is a physical-culture fanatic, has a cold bath and runs round Brixton Park every morning – which is one explanation of why he still finishes his dance with a somersault although he is over eighty.'

After the war a lot of theatres started to use the fifty-fifty system, where the management would book the band as the Top of the Bill, but the Top of the Bill would have to take a fifty-fifty share and pay the artists. The theatre management used their 50 per cent to pay the staff, lighting, and overheads. When this was first offered to Billy Cotton he was as cautious as he always was. He told Ellis that he had been offered a week's booking on this fifty-fifty system with a possible week or two following. Ellis said, 'You take it, Guv'nor, you take it' (he always called Bill Guv'nor). 'You take it, and if you go down the pan I'll go half-shares with what you lose.'

Ellis was very shrewd. They did that week, and they made a profit – and so, of course, Bill had to share that with Ellis. The next week they were booked again on the same principle, and Ellis took half the profit. The third week, Bill said, 'Well, Ellis, we've got another fifty-fifty booking, but we'll wipe out that arrangement now.'

PRACTICAL JOKER

'Bill Cotton was a great practical joker,' recalls Bill Herbert. 'His favourite stunt was to start some practical joke. He'd feel in a comedy mood, and he often took the opportunity in a stage show when several members of the band would come down front singing together in a quartet or a comedy number. While they were down front Bill would give Fred, the manager, the wink, and Fred would give Bill a jug of cold water. We had those plain wooden seats that were slightly hollow, like pub chairs, and when the fellows were down front Bill would go and tip a little water in the seats. The boys would finish, bow, take the applause, and then they would run back and sit down. Of course they were immediately sitting in water, and Bill would kill himself laughing. One time there were six or eight of us downstage, singing a hillbilly number, "Home on the Range" or something, and we had to kneel down. Bill went and got a ball of string and came behind us. While we were singing we could feel somebody fiddling at the back of us, and of course he was winding this string all round our ankles. When we stood up and went to run back, of course, we all fell arse over tip. And the band roared.

'So in return I had a joke with Billy Cotton. He had brought in a lady vocalist by then, Dolly Elsie, Jack Hylton's sister. She would sing a straight number, and then some sort of comedy number, and Bill would stand a bit to her right at the back carrying on all sorts of funny antics. Well, we were playing the Reading Palace, and the same sort of thing was still going on. As part of the equipment for aerial acts, they have holes drilled into the stage for securing the guy lines for the trapezists, which have to be very securely plugged into the stage. Bill's particular gimmick while Dolly Elsie was singing was to wander round the stage discovering the holes, put his finger down the hole, and pull it up with mock surprise, semaphoring to

Bill Herbert, Billy Cotton, and Alan Breeze in
a comedy number on stage at the Coventry
Hippodrome, 1953.

Ellis Jackson performing his dance routine.

The famous pram number with Billy Cotton
and Reg Bryant, the drummer.

the band and the stage staff, "Hole! Hole! This is dangerous!" Now, at Reading Palace the stage had rather low clearance underneath. I got a pal of mine to go down below and stand on a chair within reach of the holes I thought Bill might put his finger down. I gave him a whole jar of Brylcreem, and I told him, "Stick this jar right up against the hole." So there is Bill doing this micky-taking during Dolly's song, and I'd tipped off one or two of the band. Bill comes to a hole, and he puts his finger down it, and he pulls it up, and there is a long white icicle hanging from it. The band dried up with laughing, and he stood there, and he flung his finger round, and he said, "What the bleedin' hell is that?" Well, the band was collapsed with laughter, and he looked round to count us all and he could see that none of us were missing.

'About three months later we were travelling by train and were all sitting together in one of those open compartments, talking about something and having a damned good laugh. Old Abe, the trumpet player, was laughing so much he had to wipe his eyes with his handkerchief, and he said, "You know, I haven't laughed so much since old Bill Herbert got his mate to put that bottle of Brylcreem under the stage." The old man said, "Oh!" and he turned round and looked at me and he said, "So it was you, you bugger!" But he took it all in good part. I introduced him to my mate Jim afterwards and said, "This is the bloke who held the bottle." Bill pretended to knock him out, but he laughed.

'The drummer used to do a novelty number where he came down front with a perambulator all rigged up like a kitchen sink with dishes and saucepan lids and a big xylophone. He'd come out and do the number with Bill, smashing away at all these kitchen articles plus the xylophone. There was a pail hanging on the front of the pram. The old man got Fred to put some water in that pail, and then when old Reg, the drummer, had finished his number Bill would unhook the pail and turn round and sling the water all over him. After a time Reg got wise to it and he would dodge, and half the water would come all over us in the band. We never knew where Bill was going to sling that water.'

Comedy continued to be a prominent feature of the Billy Cotton Show as the war went on, and after the war it began to rule the roost when Dolly Elsie retired from the band to devote more time to her marriage. At this stage Bill's old friend Jimmy Phillips used his influence to diversify the show. But let Jimmy tell the story.

'I was responsible for Doreen Stephens joining the band. I said to Bill one day, "You have got to have a bit of contrast, Bill. All you are doing

57

at the moment is comedy, comedy. Why don't you get a girl singer in?"
So he brought in Doreen Stephens. She was a well-known singer in the West
End, singing in the clubs, where she had a good reputation. Then I told
Bill, "You have got to broaden the scope of the band. You have got to
start singing." "Oh, I can do that," he said. "Anyone could. I have been
singing 'Skirts' for years" (this was one of the numbers that Bill used to
sing and do a little shuffle to, during the cabaret act). I said, "Bill, it's a bit
monotonous. You have to broaden your personality." So Bill said, "What
can I do?" and I said, "Well, I will have to get you some comedy songs
to sing."

'So then I got him "Forty Fahsend Fevvers on a Frush" and similar
numbers, which Bill made quite famous in those days. Of course, his original
number, "Somebody Stole My Gal", he started playing at the Palais. Anyway, I then told Bill, "Now you have to make another change, Bill. Now
you have to start singing ballads." "I can't do that!" Bill shouted back. I
said, "You don't have to tear your heart out to sing beautifully and softly,
but it can still be a good song." The first one I got for him was "Smile",
and there was another number called "The Thing".'

Bill Cotton was changing his personality very successfully to strengthen
his impact, but the times were changing even faster, and for a short period
it seemed that the band might be drifting into the doldrums. 'When the
war ended,' Bill recalled, 'it became steadily obvious that the theatre was
taking a dive. After two years the austerity of the times seemed to hit the
people far more seriously than in the days of war, when they had cheerfully
tightened their belts. My own success fell off quite drastically. I had a very
good band, strengthened by the return of men like Frankie Kenyon, who
had been doing war work, though we mourned the loss of poor Arthur
Baker, my loyal and talented drummer, who had been killed. I spiralled
down in the general depression of live entertainment. And the failures of
the managements, who were striving desperately to get something, *anything*,
to fill the theatres, pulled me down farther. I got fewer bookings, and those
I secured were in the poorer theatres. Because it was difficult to draw in
paying audiences inside the halls, the managements began to pare their costs
by cutting the quality of the supporting acts that were on the bill with us,
and the bill was therefore less attractive.

'Variety was dying, and as often as not we would play in a theatre which,
for the two weeks previously, had shown a cheap sex play and then a nude
show. Because of the variation in the quality of the entertainment, the public
stopped coming regularly. Once they had always gone to the Hippodrome,

Alan Breeze and Doreen Stephens doing a radio
broadcast. Doreen was the band's first resident girl singer.

EIGHT LITTLE CHOIR BOYS

Words & Music by MICHAEL CARR & LEO TOWERS

2/-

Featured & Recorded on Decca Records by BILLY COTTON AND HIS BAND

The Greatest of all Comedy Songs
AIN'T LOVE GRAND

BY
LESLIE SARONY
Writer of
"Ain't it Grand to be Bloomin' Well Dead"
& RHYMES

BROADCAST AND RECORDED BY
BILLY COTTON
AND HIS BAND.

MACMELODIES
(Sole Selling Agents: Cinephonic Music Co. Ltd.,)
"DEAN HOUSE," 2, 3 & 4, DEAN STREET, W.1.

6 NET

Copyright

say, on a Thursday. It was a fixed date in their diary. Now, when the regular date included a sex play, which they did not want to see, they dropped out of the habit of constant attendance. So even when they might have wanted to see Billy Cotton, they had some other schedule.'

'WAKEY-WAKEY' IS BORN

For Billy Cotton, the dreary descent was halted by a novel decision made by someone over whom he had no control at all.

'An Australian called Jim Davidson, who was at that time assistant head of light entertainment for the BBC, was a great enthusiast for me and very much wanted to have me broadcasting for sound radio. He talked to me when I was playing at the Glasgow Empire, and he asked me if I would agree. I told him that it was impossible for me to keep a band out of work for a week. That would be the price of broadcasting under the conditions existing then, when I was picking up what theatre work I could, visiting some very out-of-the-way halls throughout the country, quite inconveniently placed for any studio. "I owe it to my boys," I told Jim Davidson, "not to put them out of regular work merely to do one broadcast. I cannot guarantee any day of the working week when I know I shall have time to get to a studio and back for my theatre performance." "Then you had better work for us on Sunday," said Jim. "How about a show on Sunday mornings?"

'Now this was absolutely revolutionary. During the war the English Sunday had departed from its usual gloom in broadcasting by accepting some lighter shows in the afternoon, and after church time in the evening (and when I refer to the English Sunday the Jocks and Taffs are not getting away with anything, because their Sabbath was far blacker than the English one). But the idea of anything like broadcast dance music in the morning was shocking. And any suggestion that the show should be provided by a crude beggar like me was even more unthinkable. But Jim Davidson had thought of it. What he had to do then was to convince other people that it was an acceptable idea. I left that particular area of persuasion entirely to him.

'Any broadcast done at this period would have to be done live, for the BBC was not yet prepared to pre-record ordinary entertainment. That was a later move which made the provision of programmes much more fluid.

'Jim Davidson carried his point, and we were booked to broadcast a trial set of six programmes at 10.30 on Sunday mornings. The first time we were on we had been playing Sunderland the preceding week. The boys and I had to come down on the overnight train, and in those days there were

ON THE TRAIL
WHERE THE
SUN HANGS LOW

by JIMMY COULTER &
JIMMY KENNEDY

Recorded & Broadcast by
BILLY COTTON
AND HIS BAND

COPYRIGHT

PETER MAURICE
MUSIC CO LTD

6ᴰ NET

very few amenities for our type of travelling. We had to arrive at the studio for rehearsal at 7 a.m. to be ready to go on the air at mid-morning. The boys had been sitting up all night in third-class carriages. After the rehearsal, when we broke before the actual performance, they just slumped where they were. I came into the studio only a few minutes before the red light was due to go on, and they were slouched around like a lot of tired giraffes. "Oi, come on," I said. *"Wakey-wakey!"* It worked, and everybody got so cheerful that the producer said that we could well start the show with it. And that was the beginning of "Wakey-Wakey".' The date of that first 'Wakey-Wakey' was 6 March 1949.

'The Sunday morning Band Show was a great success,' Bill Cotton acknowledged. 'I noticed it almost immediately in the way our theatre houses and our bookings picked up. We were soon back on number one houses only, and filling them. We went to Belfast, and they had to order out police cordons to turn the people away. My agents, Lew and Leslie Grade, then booked me and the band with Tessie O'Shea in a touring road show called "Tess and Bill". It started on a four weeks' trial, and it ran for over two years. There was no doubt that it was the Sunday radio show that was creating the demand, and when Tess and I finally split up I continued touring with the Billy Cotton Band Show and kept my ratings. The first block of six radio shows was succeeded by others of six, seven, and eight performances. Finally there came the time when for seven years without a break "Wakey-Wakey" was broadcast on sound radio for fifty-two Sundays a year.

'At the beginning there had been a certain amount of national controversy. They said we were destroying the British Sunday. Echoes of this went on for years, and I remember that a parson in Lancashire told his parishioners, "The choice is really between Billy Cotton and the Almighty, and it is you who make it." (I cannot say that I personally gave myself such high ranking.) But I was surprised by the number of clergymen who came out in support of the BBC's policy. One wrote to me while the broadcasts were still timed for 10.30, and thanked me for what I was doing on Sunday mornings. "It is a wonderful idea of the BBC's," he told me. "It cheers people up. It sends the churchgoers in to God with a different frame of mind. I know it finishes while the bells are on their last peal, but I merely delay the service until my people have time to get along, and I have told them this." "My congregation comes in," wrote another parson, "with some sort of feeling in them that Sunday is not a day of mourning. They start off in the right mood, and make it a day of happiness." After some time any direct competition with church services was removed when the show was shifted to lunch-time. That, of course, gave me a peak audience, and I did not mind if disappointed rivals called it "the soup spoon music".'

Sometimes the soup spoons that were sounding with the Billy Cotton Band Show were marking off a pretty respectable rhythm. Richard Willcocks, who produced a near-century of the radio shows, remembers the marvellous letters he used to receive from the public. 'One old gent wrote to me from Wales, and said he used to play the spoons every Sunday lunchtime while he was listening to the Billy Cotton Band Show. We put in a special song in the show and dedicated it to him and anyone else who was sitting at home at that moment playing the spoons. That's the sort of programme we were running, rough and ready perhaps, but very professional at the same time.'

EDDIE GURNEY: A THOUSAND SCRIPTS

No one has more knowledgeable memories of Billy Cotton in the great days of the radio Band Show than Eddie Gurney, who wrote a thousand scripts and nearly half as many original songs for the show.

'In my opinion Billy Cotton was unique. He got to the top and stayed at the top, and yet he had no *specific* talent as an entertainer except as an all-round show business person. He was not an instrumentalist, and the snatches of singing and dancing that he indulged in from time to time were tongue-in-cheek throwaways which were never taken seriously either by himself or by his public.

'Yet an entertainer he was. He provided a popular programme for the masses, he never pandered to the Establishment. His yardstick was always, "Would my Auntie in Wigan like it?" The logic of that simple phrase decided whether a number should or should not be included in a programme.

'Maybe Bill's greatest talent was that he could recognize talent in somebody else. If he did, he would go to great lengths to draw that someone out. There are many artists around today who found their feet through the Billy Cotton Band Show.

'I can honestly say that it was entirely through Bill that I began script writing. I had been writing the occasional comedy-cum-Dixieland number for his radio shows, then one day his script writer baled out and Bill was left dangling. It was Thursday, and he was due on the air on Sunday morning. He called me over to the Finsbury Park Empire where they were playing, and suggested that I write the following Sunday's script. I nearly passed out. I had never tried to write a script in my life and told him so. Bill said,

THE COWS IN THE MEADOW

By T. H. BINSTEAD and CLEM BERNARD

featured by BILLY COTTON AND HIS BAND

6ᴰ

Hits
FROM THE
Billy Cotton
BAND SHOW
WITH ILLUSTRATIONS

Contents

Foreword and two full pages of photographs of
BILLY COTTON IN HIS VARIOUS ROLES.

Full page photographs with their Biographies of
ALAN BREEZE, CLEM BERNARD and
DOREEN STEPHENS.

PRICE 2/6

"Look, Cocky, I think you can do it. Will you at least have a go?" Well, I had a go, and that was the start of a fifteen-year unbroken stint.

'I must be unique myself, because I am probably the only bloke to have four hundred of his compositions played over the radio: all comedy numbers, all unpublished, and all on the Billy Cotton Band Show. Add to that about a thousand scripts, as well as the fact that ultimately I played in Bill's saxophone section, and you can imagine what I feel now when someone asks, "Is it right that you used to work for Billy Cotton?"

'We cannot explain that life, that sort of routine, to people who have not experienced it themselves. It's a different world. Mind you, it was not all roses working with Bill. He could be turbulent at times. There were occasions when we had rows. There were arguments over the telephone, say when Bill had heard a playback of a broadcast and maybe a certain comedy number of mine had not quite "come off" in Bill's estimation; or I had put something in the script that had jarred him when he heard the playback. Sometimes he was right, sometimes he was wrong. But he never bore malice just as long as he believed you were sincere in your intentions towards the show. And Bill had that old adage "The Show must go on" printed through him like a stick of seaside rock.

'There were times when he would tell me, "So-and-so's ill and he won't be on the show on Sunday." And I'd say, "Blimey, Bill, now you tell me! I've already written a comedy number round him for this week." Bill would retort, "Then write another comedy number round somebody else. This show is not built on one person, mate. Even if I'm away myself, someone will have to stand in for me. When Joe Public switches on at quarter past one on Sunday, he expects entertainment, not a hard luck story."

'Sometimes people say, "Why don't you write another Billy Cotton Band Show?" And I say, "Because I can't find another Billy Cotton." Sure, I wrote the material, but it was Billy and the band, and the wonderful rapport between them, that made it all work. Several bands had a smack at doing the same type of show, but they all fell on their faces, because they had the wrong conception from the start.

'They thought it was just a matter of a few bangs and crashes, backed up by shouts and false laughter from the band. But there were a few little trade secrets that we knew and they didn't. It is my opinion that the entertainment world is a sight poorer through the passing of Billy Cotton and the subsequent break-up of his band. It was a wonderful alliance. They depended entirely on each other for their success, and it worked – for thirty-five years.'

Billy Cotton and his Band rehearsing for a broadcast in 1951.

A singer who worked with Bill Cotton for many years was Charles Young, a member of the Bandits in the radio show and of the High-Lights in the television show, with his own singing and acting roles in each. His memories are of unalloyed affection.

'The basic thing about Bill Cotton was that when you were working you *were* working, and he was a stickler for getting the job done. The good times came when we had tea-breaks. It was like a little party. All the favourites in the band used to gather around, and there was Rita [Williams] and us boys from the High-Lights – me, John McCarthy, Barney Gilbraith, and Charles Granville. We used to sit around two tables pulled together – it was a regular routine. John used to whip down first. As soon as there was a mention of a tea-break, BING, he was down, and the table prepared, and the tea was there. And this Sunday morning was really something worth looking forward to.

'Because – talking about nostalgia – there was Bill, coming out with the most amazing things, events that had happened say thirty years ago, when he and Laurie Johnson were in France, or some weird thing that had happened when they were on tour. The fantastic things they got up to! Actually remembering the particular stories they told is another thing, but the amusement that came from those Sunday morning breaks is something I can never forget. That was when Bill relaxed. He was really a very tense man. He may not have given that impression, but he wanted what he wanted, and by golly he was going to get it.

'He invariably did get what he wanted. Musically, he may not have known an E-flat from an F-sharp, but he was not musically ignorant when it came to deciding what the people wanted. This is where he would quite often say, "If I don't like it what the hell do you think Mrs Jones in Wigan will think of it?" It was the same with the script. Eddie Gurney might write something in the script, and Bill would say, "What the hell is this all about? I don't get it, and if I don't get it what chance does Mrs Brown of Tooting have? She won't get it." And, of course, he was proved right.

'In a lot of his larks he was like an overgrown schoolboy. The number of times he caught Laurie Johnson out with the "effects" hooter! POW! Right behind the ears. Well, Laurie was his nephew as well as his old friend, and perhaps he could get away with things he couldn't do to anybody else. But Laurie bore the brunt of all his schoolboy pranks, and if he could kick

The High-Lights rehearsing a number with Rita
Williams for one of the 1961 series of TV Band Shows.

him up the backside – well, this was Bill's humour. It wasn't verbal, he wasn't the most eloquent of speakers. But he was a devil at repartee.

'I'll never forget one of the anniversaries, I think it was the five-hundredth broadcast. One of the fellows brought along his wife. She was rather a grand sort of lady, and Bill of course was the reverse. He had never met her before, but she went up to him and she said, "Oh, so pleased to meet you, Mr Cotton," and then in the French style she kissed him on one cheek and then, to Bill's utter embarrassment, again on the other cheek. He looked a bit askance, as only he could. He gave her the double-take, and that was it. Later he came over to me and said, "Who the bleedin' hell was that?" He was very basic, really.

'For my part I never had a bad word with Bill, never one cross word. I had a very personal connection with him. Although I was employed by Rita, I felt I was employed by Bill. Rita could have given me the bullet any day if she had wanted to, but I used to do a solo which, of course, Bill had to pass, and I think he used to like the knowledge that I was there if Breezy was away, and consequently we had a very good relationship. It was rather nice, especially near the end, when it was necessary that he should have some people around whom he could lean on.

'He was a very big man, very heavy, but at the same time I have seen him when he used to do a head-over-heels, a cartwheel, on his stage show, until he got a bit past it. One of the funniest sights was once when Bill had to sing "Forty Fahsend Fevvers on a Frush". He was singing away, and suddenly his lower teeth came out. They fell to his waist, and he gripped them, and bunged them back in his mouth in a split second and never missed a word. If you had glanced away you would never even have seen it, it was so quick, but, of course, we were all on our knees, it was so funny.'

Michael Hurll, Bill's television producer, has a very similar story: Bill's teeth must have needed fixing. 'Bill used to get very emotional when he conducted "The Dambusters' March". That was one of our regular pieces, and he used to conduct it with his hands in front of him slightly open, fists not quite clenched. When he got to the dramatic bits in the middle he used to pound his hands very vigorously. It came to one of these spots, the band was playing, and suddenly his teeth flew out. He caught them, without stopping conducting, and put them straight back in his mouth all in one movement. The whole of the band sort of wheezed to a halt and fell about laughing. It was really funny: *da, da, da, da* – out came the teeth and straight back as if nothing had happened.'

Charles Young, a member of the Bandits and
the High-Lights for many years.

Kathie Kay, who sang with the band for twelve years.

Kathie Kay joined Bill's stage, radio, and television shows in 1957, but her memories of Bill go back much further.

'My earliest recollections of the "Guv" (the name by which Billy Cotton was affectionately known by everyone who worked for him) were when I was around six years of age. My father, a watchmaker-jeweller by profession, was also a musician of no mean ability. His taste in music encompassed all types, including the big band sounds of the day. I can remember Sunday mornings especially at our home in London when, with the radiogram on and the french windows wide open, we would be treated to one record after another, and the programme always included Billy Cotton and his band.

'So when, some years later, I was asked to come to London from my home in Scotland to join his show at the Prince of Wales Theatre, I felt at first meeting that I already knew him. His pianist, George McCallum, was at the theatre to run through my songs for inclusion in the show that night, and so there was little time for pleasantries except just introductions all round. I thought Bill's manner rather brusque. But when, at the end of the week, I had "done a good job", as he put it, he presented me with the largest box of chocolates I had ever seen, and simply said, "Thanks, Kate." This was typical of the man. He admired a worker, and he demanded only two things from his employees – loyalty and discipline. In return he was the perfect boss. It took me some time to get to know the real man, because under that tough exterior was a decidedly gentle giant with a heart as big as his build.

'He was a fair and just man, a philosopher and friend, and above all a man of unbelievable modesty. His sense of humour never let him down, and people loved him for it. He never laughed at anyone, only with them. Many times I have known him defend someone simply because life was dealing them some pretty raw deals. Like most successful people he was a tremendous judge of character. Going back to my first meeting with him, he deliberately gave you a rather hard time for a spell, and in that way he found out, simply by your reaction, what kind of person you were. If you stood up to his manner and met strength with strength, you became part of his team. He believed implicitly that a chain was as strong as its weakest link.

'I never failed to be amazed at Bill's ability to go into a studio for a broadcast – and when I joined him he had been on the air every Sunday regularly for years – and begin the morning as though it were the first one of its kind. His attention to detail at rehearsal was incredible, but when the show was on the air live for half an hour, he would then have fun and get real life into the programme.

'He often played practical jokes on us, and I vividly remember one that he pulled during a broadcast with his vocal group, the Bandits. Bill used to hand over his baton to his conductor-arranger, at that time Jackie Brown, once the show had started. He had a script to do, and it was necessary to have someone else cue the band in.

'However, when he wasn't on the mike himself, he would stroll around, either looking pleased and puffing on his cigar, or he would be in a mischievous mood, which was his way of showing you how well things were going. In this particular broadcast the group were standing at the microphone singing from their vocal copies. Bill flicked open his lighter and lit one of the parts. The flames started rising, but the group kept on singing. However, at the finish everyone just crumpled with laughter. The listeners didn't know what was happening, but Bill certainly got action and atmosphere that day!

'Sometimes our radio and TV series would be running concurrently, which meant a very late night on the Saturday and a very early start on the Sunday morning. This didn't deter Bill from taking guests to dinner after the show if it had gone particularly well. When a party of talented show-biz people get together after the work is finished, humour abounds, but Bill could usually top any humorous remarks that anyone else made. One night at the Wellington Club in Knightsbridge, which belonged to his great friends Mildred and Victor Ledger, he asked the waiter for the bill. He said, "Could I have the billet-doux, and make it out as though you were paying for it."

'When the man returned with it, Bill promptly pushed his glasses up on his forehead to study it, and this time, when he saw the amount, he said, "What's this, your telephone number?" I am sure most restaurateurs in the West End of London knew him well *and* his sense of humour. He said this sort of thing to them with a poker face, but the tip he left them was always more than generous.

'One time, when the road show was appearing in Coventry, we were all taken around the Jaguar motor works. Bill's lifelong friend Lofty England was then the boss there. Lofty used to race motor cars at the same time that Bill was also in big-time racing. They had a passion for beautiful cars, and Bill could never pass a showroom if there was something special in it. He would go in, and of course the salesman would recognize him and immediately swing into a very strong line of sales patter. Bill would say, "You've got this car for sale, mate. How much too much?" Whilst the fellow was trying to reassemble his confidence, Bill would be mentally giving the car a very experienced run-over. He'd walk all round it, open the door, sit in it, but all the time he would be saying nothing. Finally he would look the chap straight in the eye and say, "You've still got it, mate." He was a man of few words but positive action, and if in those few moments he had decided to buy the car the deal would have been closed with the same candour.

'To recount all the characteristic incidents of the twelve years that I knew Bill would fill this book. Suffice it to say that he was an unforgettable character. He flew aeroplanes, sailed yachts, raced motor cars, and remained at the top of his profession for over forty years. He packed at least four lives into one. It is to me a great privilege to have known him.'

RICHARD WILLCOCKS: 'I WAS FRIGHTENED'

Richard Willcocks came into professional contact with Billy Cotton at a very early age, and his reactions show how Bill had spanned the generations since starting in show business.

'I was twenty-three or twenty-four when I started working with Bill, after having been a radio producer for two years. The day I was asked to take over the Billy Cotton Band Show was a magical day for me. I couldn't really believe what I was being asked to do, because to me the show was a genuine institution. Possibly they thought of me because I was an amateur musician, and perhaps it seemed sensible to give the show to a producer who knew something about music.

'I remember the first time I ever met Bill. I was called into my boss's office, and there was this huge man. I'd never seen him before, and I couldn't really believe it was Billy Cotton. He said to me, "I don't mind what you do, son, providing you are careful cutting the grass."

'I was so frightened of him – or so impressed by him – that I didn't like to ask what "cutting the grass" meant. It was not until eighteen months later that I found out – it meant editing the programme. I just said, "Fine. I'll be very careful about cutting the grass." That was my first impression of him – a huge man, and I didn't understand what he was saying, but a smashing bloke, too.

'So after that meeting with him I went to produce the first show. I don't think I have ever again been so frightened as I was then. There were about thirty artists there, I suppose, with the orchestra and the singers and all the names I had heard. I had been listening to the programme since I was five

Richard Willcocks, who produced the last
ninety-nine radio Band Shows.

years old, and to hear all these characters and actually see them do it was absolutely incredible.

'I got through the first show, and then it just went on from there. I did it for about three and a half years. I did the last ninety-nine shows with Bill on radio, including the series and spectaculars for Easter and Christmas and occasions like that, big shows with guest artists. Of course, having done ninety-nine, I looked forward to doing a hundred. I had ordered the champagne myself for Bill. But we never got around to it. He died, and we never did the hundredth show.

'Working with Bill did me an awful lot of good. It taught me a great deal, it gave me professionalism, and the greatest gift of all was the understanding about what the general public wants – not just what the producer thinks they want. It is so easy to be cocky about this, and trot out your ideas of what they ought to have. But Bill had this knack of knowing what the ordinary man in the street wanted. I have lived with that ever since, and I have always tried to make my programmes in the way that I judged Bill would, too. I hope I have succeeded. But at any rate that is the effect Bill has had on me.

'I was in my early twenties when I started working with Bill, so he was considerably older than I. The way I found that I got on with him was a sort of father-and-son relationship. I could be very cheeky to him and I'd pull his leg. He used to call me son and I used to call him father, and it worked marvellously that way. He could be rude to me, too. He would tell me to get back to the cot and all that, but I suppose I came back at him, and I think the fact that I was so young and could be so rude to him too is at least one of the reasons I got on so well with him.

'The Billy Cotton Band Show was to me the essence of variety. I am a great believer in variety programmes. I always regret that we don't do so many as we used to. I used to like the broad comedy of the thing, and the sheer noise of it, which I think appeals to everyone. The great thing about the Billy Cotton Band Show was that it was utterly clean. It could be played to anybody, down to the youngest. I started listening at the age of five, and I was fairly addicted to it even at that age.

'Bill was not the greatest musician in the world, but I remember that he occasionally used to stop the recording of a song because he suddenly objected to something in it. He wouldn't be able to say, "It's those chords on the banjo, letter B." He would say, "There is a funny plinking noise somewhere in the middle." So we had to plough all the way through the arrangement whilst he was listening to it, and probably the first time through

79

he would miss it, perhaps because the banjo player had fallen asleep or something. Finally we'd find it, and he would say, "That's the bit, that's the bit," and we then had to decide what instrument it was on. But eventually we found it. And, of course, he was right. And this is really the point. He used to talk about Mr and Mrs Bolton, who were his average mister and missus, listening every Sunday. And if he didn't like it, they wouldn't like it. He was dead right every time. He used to worry about those arrangements being too fussy. Sometimes it seemed over-fussy of him to be fussy about the music, but he was dead right every time, always absolutely accurate, and that's why he was so clever.

'Of course, he put the fear in me occasionally. I was fairly frightened of him at times, as I think everybody was if they own up to it. I remember booking a studio for us to do a programme in and it didn't have a certain facility called a "talk-back facility". I suddenly thought, Oh, what am I going to say to him? I thought, I really haven't got the courage. So I went to a kind friend who was always there, Kathie Kay, and confessed, "Kathie, I have made a terrible mistake, and haven't booked a talk-back facility." Kathie said, "Never mind, I'll tell him," and she went in and told him. I went back to the box, where I sat and thought, There's going to be a huge explosion! He came into the box looking like thunder, but all he said was "You silly young beggar," and he laughed at me and went away.

'But Bill was an exceptionally generous man, generous to all the boys who played for him, and of course people were with him for years. There was one musician who had had an injury, and Bill went on paying him in spite of the fact that he was not actually playing in the band any more. One musician who was killed in the war, Bill put his son through school, paying all the fees. He was generous even down to the small things like never letting me pay for a meal, and so on. There was always a Christmas present every year for my wife, and when my second child was born my wife got the biggest bunch of flowers I have ever seen in my life. He was always like that.

'Working with Bill and all the crew, Alan Breeze – a smashing bloke – Kathie Kay and Rita Williams and the Bandits . . . oh, the memories. On my birthday Rita told Bill that was the day, and the whole band and chorus sang "Happy Birthday" absolutely out of the blue, which was a lovely moment for me but it nearly over-ran on studio time. Working with them all was really the finest reward of any programme I have done, because I felt that apart from anything else, being so young at the time, it was a marvellous link with the past. I felt I was very privileged to be involved in this

A cartoon of Billy Cotton, combining his two great loves.

Billy Cotton and Joe Brown conferring before a broadcast.

enormously professional all-fun entertainment show, which was really so good that it was basically held together by the one man and his belief that you had to entertain the public and give the public what they wanted and not what you felt they wanted. I think this is the most valuable lesson you can learn in the entertainment world, and Bill understood it better than anybody I can think of.

'When Bill went there was nobody who could replace him, especially in spending so much time encouraging young performers like Joe Brown, Cliff Richard, and Cilla Black. There was no one to help them as he had done to get a huge audience on television – and, for that matter, a fairly large one on radio.'

JOE BROWN: 'THE STUFF OF BILLY COTTON'

Richard Willcocks made an extraordinary revelation about Billy Cotton's thoughts on who had the personality to be his successor: 'One of the occasional guests we had on the radio show was Joe Brown. He was always good value, and he filled the spot beautifully. I remember Bill telling me that if anything ever happened to him, the person who should take over his role in that world should be Joe Brown. He had marvellous respect for Joe Brown. Joe had a young, sort of cheeky attitude to Bill, and I think that is the reason why they got on so well.'

Joe Brown's own reaction to Billy Cotton is therefore of more than ordinary interest. And again it began with familiarity with the Band Show from the days of the radio broadcasts.

'I first became aware of Bill Cotton when I was a kid, and I had a winkle round [that is, going round with a barrow selling winkles]. I used to go round the East End on Saturday morning and afternoon and on a Sunday morning. I always remembered Bill because when the Band Show used to come on, that was the time I would be in my back kitchen in the pub, with all the left-over winkles and shrimps that we couldn't sell mixed up with all the money – and as we were counting the money, me and my mate would sit there eating all the shrimps and winkles we had left.

'Later on, after I had come into this business, I was doing a record "plug" and they asked me if I would come along and do the Billy Cotton Band Show. Being a sort of young groovey and all at that time, I thought to myself, Cor, I'm not doing that – I remember that when I was a kid, it can't be anything to do with me now. Anyway, there was a bit of an argument, and my manager said, "Well, you've got to do it. I've booked it. Go on up to the BBC."

83

'So I went along, and I think from that day I was really hooked on the Billy Cotton sort of thing, because it was so bloody humorous and so tongue-in-cheek that you had to be there in the middle of it or you'd never believe it. It never used to come over to me like that, that this was what it was all about, and all the blokes in that band had been with him for years and years, and old Alan Breeze would be there, and that old guy Bill Herbert, who used to come out with that trolley with all the bloody doors and bells on.

'Anyway, we did our little plug, and Bill was knocked out with it. He thought it was great, and he said, "Well, let's see you on the show again." So we came again, and this time we played some little bits of jazz stuff, which was more in keeping with the show. We did "Won't You Come Home, Bill Bailey" and a few things like that, and Bill was really knocked out with it.

'He used to rule that band with a rod of iron. You've never seen anything like it. But, you know, you couldn't get one of those guys, not one of them, to say a bad word against Billy Cotton. That's a funny thing, because hard-bitten musicians have generally got no respect at all for people who don't take musicians seriously, and to a certain extent old Bill used to do that. I don't think he was a particularly good musician, he didn't read very well. But you'd always hear them say something like, "Ah, yes, but he has a good ear." They had a tremendous amount of respect for him as a man, and of course when he was younger he had been a bit of a tearaway, racing motor-bikes and motor cars and flying aeroplanes: he was a power-boat driver then.

'Anyway, we did about five of these shows, and one day Bill said to me, "Look, you turn up any time you want to do a plug. You just turn up here and do it – right?" I turned up one day right out of the blue, and Bill imme-diately said, "Right, we're pulling this number out and that number out to let young Joey do his bit" (that's what he used to call me, young Joey). Well, that caused a powerful row with the producer. And Bill bawled him out on my behalf in front of the band. I don't think he has ever forgotten that.

'After that I got to meet Kathie Kay, and when I did a summer season at Great Yarmouth I stayed in Alan Breeze's cottage, and I used to go down with him several times to see Bill, and I got to know Kathie and her son, I was great pals with them.

'As for Bill, he was great. A great bloke. A really rough bloody nut, you know, but one of the greatest Cockney gentlemen that I have ever met.

'I always liked the radio show in preference to the television. There was

Cliff Richard always enjoyed his appearances on the show.
BBC COPYRIGHT

THE
BILLY COTTON
BAND SHOW

SUNDAY 1.30 PM
LIGHT PROGRAMME

never any smut, of course, not in either, and I think Billy Cotton deserves a lot of acclaim for setting a standard. Of course, old Breezy and that lot were right loonies. When you can see them reading it as opposed to hearing them read it on the wireless, when you are watching them read it all, it's a bit like "The Goon Show". It's all innuendoes. Like when they say a gag that they have never even seen before – phew, it's only then that they realize how bad it is. That's how all those things crept in about the script writer originally. They'd say, "What's he got for us this week, what's he written now?" and it would be part of the show. To me it was great. I remember a lovely script that always turned me on, when old Bill was reading his lines and he said, "Now, then, Breezy, what have you got for us this week?" And Breezy comes up with a very hoarse throat, and he says, "I'm afraid I can't sing this week, Bill. I've got a sore throat." Bill says, "Have you never tried Dr Benjamin's throat lozenges?" Breezy says, "No," and Bill says, "'Ere you are, Breezy, have one." Breezy apparently takes one, pops it into his mouth, "la-la's" up and down the scale – and then starts off singing like a bird.

'Ah, it was an incredible show, and he was a great humorist, a true professional, and the salt of the earth. During my career, for what it's worth, I remember certain people with a great amount of respect, and Bill Cotton is one of four, really. In the old days everybody loved a comic, and Bill was a true comic all right, even without opening his bloody mouth, and there is not many you can say that about. I would put him on a par with Jimmy Wheeler and Bud Flanagan.

'Ah, Bill. It's my belief that he never got the acclaim he deserved. Just a real great bloke.'

THE GENUINE GURNEY

Everybody who talks about Billy Cotton refers to the twenty years of regular radio programmes in terms which almost imply that they were brainwashed by them. And maybe they were. Let's revive some memories of what actually went on as far as the words are concerned – you will have to play your own records to remember the music: or perhaps your own nostalgia, your own tunes-in-the-mind, is better than any scratched record. Here is a taste of what it used to be, excerpts from Eddie Gurney's script for Billy Cotton's Five-Hundredth Radio Band Show, transmitted on Sunday 29 April 1962 between 1.30 and 2.00 p.m. on the Light Programme. The billing announces:

Stubby Kaye and Billy Cotton dancing the 'If
You're Light on Your Feet' routine.
BBC COPYRIGHT

THE 500th BILLY COTTON BAND SHOW

BILLY COTTON
introduces
ALAN BREEZE
KATHIE KAY
RITA WILLIAMS AND THE BANDITS
THE COTTON CHOIR
THE BILLY COTTON BAND
Conductor: Jackie Brown

AND GUESTS
HARRY SECOMBE: PEGGY MOUNT: ADAM FAITH

Script by Eddie Gurney
F/X by Laurie Johnson
Produced by Eric Miller

'F/X' is the studio shorthand for 'Effects', and Laurie Johnson, Bill's nephew, was the man, as Charles Young recalled, who was always getting it POW! behind the ears when Billy Cotton caught him from behind. You can tell the speed with which the performances were put on: though the broadcast was timed for 1.30 p.m. on Sunday, the rehearsal only began at 9.30 on the same morning. The studio was the Piccadilly Theatre in Lower Regent Street, and the stage manager was Joe Young.

The programme followed 'Two-Way Family Favourites', as it was then called, and the introduction for this celebration show was made, not by a continuity announcer, but by Jean Metcalfe from her own 'Family Favourites' studio:

'And now, having said good-bye to one Bill, it's time to say hello to another. *This* Bill is celebrating his five-hundredth birthday today, and he's invited Peggy Mount, Adam Faith, and Harry Secombe, together with a studio audience to join in the fun. I'm sure you'll know who I'm referring to, the moment you hear that soft sweet voice of his calling ...'

'WAKEY-WAKEY!' Billy Cotton comes in loud and clear from the Piccadilly studio. And over the applause the band plays 'Somebody Stole My Gal'.

Over the band Bill Cotton breaks in with, 'All right, all right – that's enough. Good afternoon, everybody. This is Billy Cotton introducing another Billy Cotton Band Show. As for you, Jean Metcalfe, I'll have you know it's me five-hundredth *broadcast*, not me five-hundredth *birthday!* Bloomin' cheek! How about that husband of yours – Cliff Michelmore? How many of those television shows has *he* done? So how old does that make *him*!!!' Cotton sounds as if he is laboriously thinking: 'What do they call that programme of his? "S'mornin' '...? "S'arternoon"...?'

A shout comes over from Michael John, who has succeeded Barney Gilbraith in the Bandits and the High-Lights (all these singers had to work on the comedy, too): 'No, yer twinny! "*Tonight*"!'

'That's it,' says Bill. 'Tonight's tonight, and tomorrow night'll be tonight tomorrow night. I hope I make myself clear.'

The singers and the band immediately launch into Leonard Bernstein's song 'Tonight' from *West Side Story*.

Over the applause Bill announces, 'That was "Tonight", featuring Rita Williams and the Bandits. And now I'd like to present Alan Breeze. Breezy, like most of the lads on this stage today, has been with me a mighty long time. Just how long is it, son?'

'O-oh ...' says Breezy. 'Approximately, William, I would say since the year 200 BBC!'

'How time flies!' sighs Bill. 'To me it doesn't seem a day over eighty-five years. Go on, sing, mate.'

Alan Breeze and the band sing a specially written song, 'The Year 200 BBC'.

'Jolly good,' concedes Bill when it's over. 'Let's see, who's next? Ah, it's Kathie Kay. Do you remember the first Sunday you sang with the show, Kate?'

'Gosh, yes, Bill,' gushes Kathie. 'Was I nervous!'

'That's right,' Bill remembers. 'So I took you round the corner and bought you a drink, didn't I?'

Kathie considers the memory for a moment and replies, without relish, 'Yes...a pint of bitter. And when I said I'd prefer a cocktail you said, "O.K." – and stuck a cherry in it.'

'Well, I always say,' Bill remarks easily, 'if you're having a drink, you might as well have what you want. Come on, what are you going to sing for us?'

'"She's Got You",' Kathie announces.

'Fine,' says Bill.

The band come in and Kathie sings. As Bill is thanking her, Laurie Johnson on 'effects' puts in the sound of a door opening. Charles Young, apparently just entering, does a double-take on seeing the audience and says craftily,

90

Bill and Kathie Kay handing out presents at a
Christmas party in the studio.

Adam Faith was another guest on both radio and television.

'Oi! 'Allo, so you've got an audience today, have you?'

'Yes,' says Bill, 'it's me five-hundredth broadcast.'

'I see,' says Charles Young with understanding. 'And I suppose they've come along so that you can apologize in *person* to 'em for the other 499!'

Bill roars out his expected ritual shout of 'GETOUTOFIT!'

'Don't worry, I'm going. Good morning,' Charles Young assures him, and he fades away singing, 'Oh, they've been together now for five hundred years.'

Laurie Johnson crashes in the effect of a door slamming.

'Well, maybe we have . . . or nearly,' says Bill resignedly. 'But that doesn't stop us recognizing real talent when we hear it. And the young man I'm going to introduce to you has certainly got plenty of that. He's appeared with us on television – and I'd like to say right now that it was a great pleasure working with him. That is why I asked him if he'd appear with us again today . . . and here he is, to sing "As You Like It". Ladies and gentlemen – Adam Faith!'

Adam Faith sings his song with the band, and Bill thanks him. 'Adam, son, that was great.'

'I was hoping it would be "as you like it", Bill,' says Adam.

'No doubt about that, mate, it certainly was,' Bill assures him. 'And many thanks for coming.'

'A pleasure,' Adam replies. 'And, say – don't forget to invite me along when you celebrate the next five hundred!'

'Blimey,' says Bill, 'we hope to see you long before then.'

'Oh, I expect you will. So long, Bill.'

'So long, Adam.' And Adam Faith goes off to applause which is topped by the agitated voice of Rita Williams in her 'Mrs Spiegel' spot.

'Mr Cotton,' she interrupts, very breathless. 'Mr Cotton – wasn't that Adam Faith?'

'It was,' Billy confirms. 'And he's just sung a smashing song. Pity you missed it.'

'Say,' demands Rita. 'When are you going to let mein Eddie sing? He's got the loudest 'obsons what you've ever heard! At home, you can stand in the conservatory and hear him singing in the bathroom – even if you're in the next street.'

'Shut up! Shut up!' interrupts sax-player Eddie Spiegel, who is the regular butt of this spot. 'Why don't you be quiet, woman? Every time you open your mouth I feel like putting *my* foot in it!'

'Why don't you two buzz off,' Billy Cotton pleads, 'and let us get on

The Variety Club's 1962 Show Business
Awards: Violet Carson, Billy Cotton, Sheila
Hancock, and Leslie Caron.

with the next number – which happens to be "Deep Purple" played as a trumpet solo by Grisha Farfel.'

Grisha plays his popular trumpet solo, with vocal and orchestration arrangement, and Bill thanks him and the Cotton Choir.

'Well,' Bill continues, 'now Kathie Kay joins me in a little duet entitled "Let's Not Be Sensible". As a matter of fact, this is where Peggy Mount should have appeared, but I don't know where she's got to.'

At this the well-known voice of Peggy Mount booms, 'What do you mean, you don't know where I've got to!!! I've been sitting down there among the audience waiting to be called.'

'Blimey!' says Bill in mock astonishment. 'It – it – it's Peggy Mount!' And as the audience applauds, he greets her. 'Hello, Peggy, how are you, love? I'm very sorry, but I didn't see you sitting there.'

'Course you didn't!' storms Peggy. 'You're all so flaming busy. What with you waving your arms at the band – and the band making rude signs back at *you*!'

'Anyway, now that you *are* here, Peggy,' says Bill soothingly, 'what are you going to do for us?'

'Well, Bill,' Peggy confesses, softening, 'at heart I suppose I'm just like thousands of others. I'd love to be a singer!'

'What, *you*?' interrupts Billy in spontaneous amazement.

'Yes,' says Peggy defensively, and she goes on the warpath: 'And why shouldn't I? I'll bet I can put as much tenderness and sweetness into a song as any of your Tommy Faiths and Adam Steeles, any day.'

After some palaver Peggy is coaxed into starting a duet with Bill, after insisting, 'Tell 'em to keep it *down*. The trouble with you is you're such a noisy lot.'

The song has not got far before Bill stops and says, 'Yes, Peggy, yes. It's very nice, but ...'

'But what?'

'Well, I'm not sure how to put it, but your *diction* isn't quite ...'

Peggy drops her Cockney character voice and comes in icily with her normal voice: 'And what, pray, is wrong with the diction?'

''Ere,' Bill protests in surprise, 'you talked altogether different then. Is *that* your proper voice?'

'Of course it's my proper voice,' says Peggy, pretty upper-class. Then she relapses into Cockney:

'I only use *this* one when I'm working, you clot!'

'Hm,' says Bill reflectively, and puts on his own exaggeration of a snooty voice: 'Now you come to mention it, Miss Mount, I don't use *my* normal 'obsons when I'm working on the stage.'

'Bill,' says Peggy with the kindest severity, 'if that's a sample of it, I don't blame you.'

Bill immediately flashes into his stage, looking-for-trouble voice. 'Oh, yer don't, don't yer? And what's wrong with it?'

Peggy is back in Cockney character: 'It reminds me of Jimmy Wheeler playing Henry V – that's what's wrong with it. Here, I say, is that the *time*? Heavens! I've just remembered I left the cabbage on boiling! Bill, I must dash.'

Bill sees Peggy off affectionately, and she urges, 'Go on, you two, get on with your duet, don't let me stop you. Ta ta.' Bill and Kate sing their delayed 'Let's Not Be Sensible'. The next number is Harry Secombe's spot, which for this performance is on tape. Billy expresses his thanks, and the gramophone 'effects' whirl in with the flying saucer sound. For this is the regular 'You down there with the glasses' interlude, with Charles Granville as the Space Man.

'Hey you!' calls Charles Granville. 'You down there with the glasses! That was a strange invitation you sent me to come along as a guest on this show!'

'What was wrong with it?' asks Bill.

'Well,' says the Space Man aggressively. '*Guest* is not spelt p-e-s-t.'

'In your case, it is,' says Bill.

'Five hundred shows!' mutters the Space Man. 'And not one kind word. I guess *my* record is better than yours. So long, I'll be seeing you.' And the grams roll out the 'flying saucer exit' effect.

'Having got rid of *him*,' Bill announces with relief, 'we come now to our final number. It's our arrangement of *Porgy and Bess*, and it features the band, the singers, in fact the whole bloomin' issue. And here it is.'

The band and singers put over a medley of 'I've Got Plenty of Nothing', 'Bess, You Is My Woman', 'It Ain't Necessarily So', and 'Summertime', and the grams throw in a final crash over the applause which is explained as the kitchen sink, since everything else had been put in.

'Well,' says Bill, 'that, ladies and gentlemen, concludes the show for today. So on behalf of all of us here in the studio, including our producer Eric Miller* – and I don't know where *he* is. Last night, after our television show, I introduced him to the Silhouettes; nobody's seen him since!!! This is Billy

*Over the years the show had many producers. In addition to Eric Miller and Richard Willcocks, who is mentioned earlier, they included Glyn Jones, Richard Dingley, Johnny Kingdom, and John Forsythe Wilson.

Cotton saying, "Cheerio for now," and don't forget – WAKEY-WAKEY!!!' The band breaks into 'Somebody Stole My Gal'. Bill adds, 'Well, they say the first five hundred broadcasts are the hardest, so it looks as if we've broken the back of it!' And he thanks the backroom boys of the production, calls loudly, 'Right, Joe – beat it in, son,' the band plays 'Legion Patrol', and the show is over.

ROYAL COMMANDS

In 1950 Billy Cotton was commanded to appear with his band in the Royal Command Performance at the London Palladium, the last to be attended by King George VI. The people he took to the Palladium were the kernel of his post-war orchestra. His vocalists were Alan Breeze and Doreen Stephens. Laurie Johnson took violin and banjo. On saxophone Bill had Frankie Kenyon, Charles Swinnerton, Stan Quiddington, and Eddie Spiegel, with Alfie Reece and Rube Stoloff on trombones, and Eddie Lever, Lew Dunn, and Ray Landis on trumpets. The pianist and arranger was the tireless Clem Bernard; Bill Herbert, on guitar, took over the piano when Clem was engaged in a comedy spot. Eric Field played bass and Reg Bryant was on drums. Two years later Bill was at the Palladium again for the first Royal Command Performance before the present Queen. Slight changes in the band put Wilbur Jones in for Stan Quiddington on sax, Eddie Lever had left the trumpet section, and Grisha Farfel and Ernie Fearn were in, while Frank Wilson replaced Rube Stoloff on trombone. Ellis Jackson was in and out of the band all through the years.

Altogether, Billy Cotton appeared in five Royal Command Performances, including one at the Victoria Palace. But in addition to that, because he was a great personal favourite of the Royal Family, he was often asked to play at Windsor Castle for the Royal Household Christmas Party, which, although it was a big function, was still a much more intimate affair held in the Waterloo Chamber. Bill Herbert remembers, 'At the last party at Windsor, I was asked to go and be presented to the Queen and then the Queen Mother. The Queen Mother said to me, "We love Billy Cotton's Band. He *is* jolly, isn't he?" I said, "Yes, Ma'am. But *you* haven't got such a good aim as you used to have. You remember the last Command Performance we did at the Palladium, when we came to 'I've Got a Loverly Bunch of Coconuts', the comic gang climbed up to your box and gave you half a dozen snowballs. And you stood up and threw one and hit me, *bang*, right alongside of my nose. But you didn't do that tonight." The Queen Mother roared with laughter and said, "I'm a rotten shot now."

97

Billy Cotton rehearsing for the Royal
Command Performance at the Victoria Palace
Theatre in 1960.

Spot the Stars! Dress rehearsal of the finale for
the Royal Command Performance of 1960.

'The Queen was very beautiful and I'm very proud to have shaken hands with her. Prince Charles came up and had a chat about the guitar, and Princess Margaret was very jolly. She said to me, "What was jazz like in the old days?" I said, "Well, you know the Temperance Seven?" She laughed and said, "Yes." "Well," I said, "we used to play like that. But we meant it. It was serious."'

Kathie Kay appeared at three Royal Command Performances, and two Christmas Parties at Windsor. 'The very last show we did at the Castle, we were told that the show would be a certain length, and that all the Royal Family would be there except Prince Philip, who was away. If Her Majesty the Queen tired, she would not wait until the end, she would just get up and leave. However, she did not leave, which I suppose was a compliment to us all. When the snowballs were being thrown in the "Coconuts" number, one of the snowballs actually hit her tiara and sent it askew. Bill thought that was great, but he apologized to her afterwards, and she didn't mind at all. We were all invited to go into a smaller room leading out of the ball-room, where they would come and talk to us for a while, but we actually spent two hours there. Prince Charles was at that time learning Welsh. Our drummer then was a Welshman, Wally Thompson, so they got on famously, and the Prince wanted to come and play the drums. I think the Royal Family always choose the people they want to see for a Household Party, and they did regard Bill's show as family entertainment. They liked him, they just liked his perky sense of humour.'

Peter Brough, who used to organize the Royal Household parties, also remembers the snowball incident when Bill hit the Queen's tiara. 'There was great laughter over this, and many apologies and forgiveness afterwards.' But he also gives a lively instance of Bill's 'perky sense of humour': 'When the introductions were being made to the Queen, Her Majesty asked if she could hold Archie Andrews. As she got hold of him his head fell off. Bill Cotton, who was standing nearby, said, "I bet that's the first one you've beheaded in your time."'

Michael Hurll, who started as floor assistant on Billy Cotton's first show for BBC Television and finished as his producer, went to the last Windsor Party, and tells a moving but extremely comic story of Bill Cotton's stiff memory in his seventieth year. 'Bill's stage show was like Pavlov's dogs, it started, and followed a steady pattern which was always the same, and went through to the end. After the trumpet feature came Kathie Kay, so you knew that once he said, "Thank you very much, Grisha Farfel," he would follow it up immediately with, "And now for our little lady of song

Peter Brough and Archie Andrews.

– Kathie Kay." But when we went to Windsor Castle we put in two other acts: John Tremaine, a mind reader who was very popular at the time, and also Ken Dodd as a top of the bill. So the Queen is sitting there, and the Queen Mother and everybody, and we get to the end of the trumpet player's number. Then Bill said, "Thank you very much, Grisha Farfel, and now here's our little lady of song."

'But a couple of fellows in the band prompted, "No, no. It's the mind reader." There were big stage whispers, and Bill said, "WHAT?" They said, "No, it's not Kathie, it's the mind reader." Bill said, "I bloody announced her, and she's bloody coming on." All this in front of the Queen and the Queen Mother. "Ladies and gentlemen, Kathie Kay," he announced. And they loved it, the Royal Family, they absolutely loved it. But that's what he could do. He could get away with things like that. He was a particular favourite of the Queen Mother's. She loved the Billy Cotton Show.'

EARLY TELEVISION

In the early days of television Billy Cotton deliberately fought shy of the medium. 'With few exceptions, I kept away from it. Apart from appearing in one or two gala programmes – to celebrate the Coronation and the Queen's return from Australia – I would not appear. This was a blunt commercial decision of mine. As long as there was no rival service and the BBC had the monopoly, the fees offered were unrealistically low. For the money that was offered I could not afford to build programmes which had to be jettisoned as soon as they were seen.

'When Independent Television burst upon the scene my own agents, Lew and Leslie Grade, were deeply involved in the management side. They realized that one of their primary concerns would be to provide real live entertainment. What they had already available must be immediately mustered and assembled in full marching order, complete with ammunition, and report for duty. I was one of their advance units. We went on and did a lot of numbers that were our property from the stage shows, and we adapted broadcast numbers to make them fit for TV stage presentation. I candidly thought they were under-rehearsed and far too elaborately produced for my basically very simple type of show.

'All this was vividly illustrated in a climax of confusion which occurred when a great hunting scene was devised as the finale to a programme. The George Mitchell Singers were in on it, the girls in black riding-habits, the boys in hunting pink. They were to sing "John Peel". Four of my brass players were given four-foot-long post horns, and the rest of my band were in the act too. I was to be seated on Goldie, the wonder horse, the lovely palomino hired from Vera Cody. To complete the picture postcard finale, a great load of beagles was to be thrown on the stage. And, to the singing, the post-horning, the supporting brass, the horse Goldie with Billy Cotton up, and the yapping of a pack of hounds – the great scene would end.

'At the rehearsal of this number it was noticed that the hounds were rather bored. Instead of looking keen as mustard, as if John Peel had already cried, "View-hallo!" in the next field, they were wandering in a very friendly fashion about the stage, sniffing at the drums, very much at ease but not what you could call eager. After rehearsal, someone had the bright idea of concentrating the hounds in the middle of the picture by rubbing aniseed on the bottoms of the trousers of the bandsmen in the middle group. The idea was that the aniseed would confine the hounds' curiosity to the part of the stage that was scented. There was no dummy run for this manœuvre – and the chap in charge of the aniseed got his prescription wrong and wildly over-anointed the bandsmen's trousers.

'The great moment came. I heaved myself astride Goldie. The hunting types went on. The post horns were raised, and "D'Ye Ken John Peel" came over big and strong. Then they released the hounds. Ten pairs of beagles came streaking across the stage straight for the bandsmen's trousers. They swarmed around them and then lifted their legs and watered the serge, all the time yapping with an excitement that indicated that this was the best beagles' orgy that had ever been set up for them. The cameras were hastily hauled up above dog level – (there was still me on a horse and the tops of four post horns to concentrate the interest on), and the great British public never had such a spectacle, or such a laugh, as we provided with that particular show.

'I finished that ITV series in a very dissatisfied frame of mind, though my managers were offering me more money and longer time. I enjoyed the friendship of the BBC's head of light entertainment, Ronnie Waldman, and one day I asked him, "Will you do a deal with me if I leave ITV?" He said, "Well, Bill, I think I know you well enough to say this. You're not playing me against them, are you?" "I'm doing nothing of the sort," I replied. "I have made up my mind, and I am willing to come to the BBC because in my opinion you have more experience in this television lark. I've worked all these years for BBC Sound. I've always had a square deal."

'Ronnie Waldman said, "Let's get down to it now. Come out to lunch." We went to the little Bertorelli's that was by Shepherds Bush Green. Before I knew where I was he had his pencil out and was saying, "Let's write down here how much money you want. For a three-year exclusive contract. We can tie the Sound and TV together."

'They had paper napkins on the table. I took his pencil and I wrote down a figure on a napkin. It was a large sum of money, more than the BBC had ever paid anyone else. I said, "Don't look at it now. Don't spoil your lunch. Wait till the meal is over." But Ronnie opened the paper immediately, read the figure, and said, "It's a deal." He looked as cool as ever, but I believe he had a hard job talking the BBC into accepting it.

'It was not an outrageous demand, though. I was saying to Ronnie, "Accept it, and I am a BBC man. My career is now in BBC Television and Radio. Slot me in to do what theatre work I can do, but from now on everything else is an 'also ran'." The money I was asking would make it possible for me to keep my band together and to offer them a security that no band-leader can normally offer his boys. And that paper napkin, which I marked in 1957, was and continued to be my only contract with the BBC for all the happy times afterwards.'

Ronnie Waldman well remembers that lunch at Bertorelli's – though not that Bill produced a settled figure almost off the top of his head. After all, Bill did not know that Ronnie would come straight out with a proposal for a sound and vision package deal – and neither did Ronnie at the beginning of the conversation, for he had not even talked to the radio people. 'I took a chance,' Ronnie says. 'I would commit the sound people because I wanted Bill for television. I asked him what he wanted. He pulled the paper napkin over and started scribbling, adding, subtracting, and multiplying. He shoved the paper over to me and said, "That is the figure." I said, "Done!" and that was it. It was as simple as that. But I then had to come back and have a hell of a fight with the BBC to get it through.

'But really, it was not much of a fight. We all knew that Bill was, with his band, the greatest entertainer almost bar none. Who at that time could produce shows that attracted such enormous audiences and such a wide age range? In my own case, my mother, who I think was then in her seventies, and my son, who was four or five, were equally devoted to him. My son insisted on going to every rehearsal of the Billy Cotton Band Show at the theatre, because he worshipped Bill. He thought he was the most wonderful man he had ever seen. And so did I, frankly. And that was the simple story.

'As head of light entertainment I was what I suppose nowadays would be called executive producer. I knew what I wanted to see on the screen, and I was fortunate enough to have two producers, one after the other, who knew exactly what *they* wanted to see on the screen, and it was the same as what I wanted and the same as what Bill wanted. So there was never any problem. Those producers were Brian Tesler and young Bill Cotton, and you can't do better than that. They did an absolutely superb job with the show, especially considering that we started at a time when our equipment and our techniques were still a bit rough. (They improved rapidly, of course, but in the early days cameras were not so good as later, and so on.)

'They laid out the conventions, such as the start of the shows. They built the idea of the girls doing the opening number with him, and then he did his yell at them, "GETOUTOFIT!" – and the girls rushed off. They developed Bill's announcement, which he was always quite happy to do, although he always swore that he was going to forget what he had to say.

'As a man Billy Cotton was an all-round great. He was a great racing driver, a great boat-lover, a great carer for his men. Their welfare was always in the forefront of his mind. That contract we worked out was what was best for them – not what he needed, but what they needed to maintain their standard of living. Bill was robust, rumbustious, honest beyond any man I have known in my life, with an instinct for entertainment which very few people have ever equalled. He was a great companion, but also a great worrier – some of his illness was the result of the considerable amount of worry he had in his life. But he was a man I'd rather be with than with practically anyone else I've ever met.

'The deep quality of his show was that it was enjoyable to a range of people of whom some would never even admit that they found it enjoyable. It put over a sense that the performers themselves really liked working with Bill – and of course there was no question about that. And Bill enjoyed what he was doing, though it was very hard work. He had this incredibly powerful instinct for building a show in which the pacing was absolutely right. He didn't have to *think* any more about how to put a show together, how to choose the numbers, or to remember to balance the keys. I wish modern disc jockeys would think more about that to make their shows more attractive. But they don't even realize it. Bill knew all these things eventually by instinct – that you don't put three items together all in the key of E-flat, or all in the same tempo. Building a show with Bill was a great exercise in instinctive show business.'

TELEVISION BREAKTHROUGH

After Billy had signed his contract with the BBC he fulfilled the touring engagements to which he was already committed, and brought the band

Ronnie Waldman was responsible for securing
Billy Cotton and his Band for BBC Television.

in for 'limbering up' television shows when he was playing theatres near London. He compered a television series called 'Tin Pan Alley' with which he was not very happy, and the series was taken off. Ronnie Waldman was now ready for the big take-off. Bill always remembered what he thought was the unpromising introduction to this.

'Ronnie said, "I've got a university boy who has just left Cambridge, and I want you to work with him." I said, "What do you expect me to do with a university boy from Cambridge?" He said, "I'm hoping you're going to get the biggest shock of your life. Together, you and he are going to do things in television that you never imagined. Together. *You*, because you know; you're a professional. *He*, because he has an enormous capacity for getting the unexpected out of any production he takes on. He has been through the school here. I've watched him. He is a protégé of mine, and I don't get paid to make mistakes. Bear with me and have a go."

'That was the conversation that launched the Billy Cotton Band Shows on television. I turned up for the first rehearsal, and I met the boy from Cambridge, who said to me, "I am Brian Tesler. Come along and meet the others." The first person I saw was Leslie Roberts, who had produced a lot of cabaret shows. He had brought along a line of dancing girls (soon to become famous as the Silhouettes). I looked at these girls and I said, "Gawd! For me? What am I supposed to be – Anton Dolin?" Leslie Roberts came up. "What am I doing here?" I asked him. "I can't dance, and at my time of life I don't see myself starting to learn." He said, "We're going to try and cultivate this line of girls with you." "Well," I said, softening a bit, "perhaps I could learn." "Of course you can," said Tesler. "Show me," I said to Roberts. He said, "I'm hoping that you are going to like these girls so much that you will join in with them. I'll make it as easy as possible." We started to rehearse. And I started to learn.

'It was forty years since, with the crossed swords of the Army School of Gymnastics on my arm, I used to put my sweating fellow-officers from the Number 16 Squadron, Royal Flying Corps, through their paces at early morning physical training. Now I was to know exactly how they had felt. I took the challenge, and I refused to short-cut any of the skill of getting the steps right. The choreographer said that it was because I still had the sense of balance that I had used as a boxer and gymnast and footballer that I could manage these complicated routines. Sometimes they thought they would do me a favour by passing me the easy bits or suggesting that I should be "masked" in some intricate step. But I have always known that you can't kid the public, not all of them. I wanted it to be right. "I'm not earning the bloody money!" I used to roar if they tried to leave me out. I felt that if it was a part of my act as an entertainer to do these dance routines, I should not get away with less than the script demanded. I used to come in early every day for dance rehearsals with the girls. And I would take the head girl aside to get the most complicated steps right. So when I later brought onto my show Stubby Kaye – the great entertainer who also became my great friend – and we did a number reasonably well together, it was quite just that the title of the dance routine should be "If You're Light on Your Feet".

'One of the greatest compliments I have ever received was a report in the *Dancing Times* which read: "It takes a bandleader of sixty to show the British dancing public what a *pas de deux* should be. Is there some mistake, and has Billy Cotton been a professor all this time?" It was a new and rewarding activity for me to do these numbers in the show with the Silhouettes. They were wonderful girls, very keen on their jobs, and a very nice type of girl. Their line-up when they came with me to the Royal Command Variety Performance of 1960 at the Victoria Palace, when my son Bill Junior produced our "Wakey-Wakey Tavern", was: Maura Bowes, Jo Cook, Hazel Hepworth, Pat Hughes, Wendy Murphy, Coral Reynolds, Brenda Ross, Maureen Rudd, Rita Scrivener, Audrey Spurden, Candy Scott and Betty Walker.'

BRIAN TESLER GETS CRACKING

Brian Tesler had served four years with Ronnie Waldman's BBC Light Entertainment department when he was introduced to Billy Cotton.

'My reaction when first asked to produce the Band Show was one of surprise that I should be thought of, and then of considerable excitement as I came to see the possibilities. I went to see Bill in music hall, and saw what a vibrant show he put on with the band and the singers. It was boisterous, and very funny. As I watched the band on the stage I could see ways in which we could use their production numbers for television. Then I thought we could bring in dancers to dance with Bill. He could obviously do little routines, and the juxtaposition of this large man – who, like many large men, was capable of delicate and dainty movements – with a bunch of beautiful and glamorously dressed showgirl dancers would obviously be very appealing. And it was.

'We did a sort of pilot single show in which I put in some of the ideas that had come to me while watching the stage show. We did use some of their material, we brought in the girls, and we did some purely television

Brian Tesler was the first producer of the TV
Band Shows, and had much to do with
deciding how the show was finally presented.

The Silhouettes performing a precision number.

things in terms of production that can't be done on the stage. The Silhouettes were actually called that because we used a technique called "overlay and inlay" (which is now, since the advent of colour, called Chromakey) in which you can take a person's silhouette and fill it with anything you want: newsprint, for example, so that it looks like newspaper figures dancing over the clouds or whatever. It was a technique I developed at the BBC, it was very effective, and that's why we called the girls the Silhouettes. What I missed most after leaving the BBC was Bill, and the band, and the girls, and often during the following years I used to go back and see the show, and go out for a meal with Bill and young Bill.

'That first show had all the boisterousness of the Cotton music hall appearances. It was very successful, and it was clear that we could build a good television series on these lines. I got an old friend, Jimmy Grafton, to write the link pieces and supply some of the ideas. We would work it out together with Bill. I would go for a programme discussion to his office in Denmark Street – a very small office where he used to sit in an enormous high-backed antique chair. Bill would chip in with ideas of his own that would embellish what I was suggesting, because he could reach back into his memory for a routine that his band had done and that would fit in with the idea under discussion.

'Then we would break for lunch and go to one or other of his favourite Italian restaurants in Soho – Isola Bella or Leoni's. He loved going to Italian restaurants, but he would never order Italian food. The place would have to be prepared to supply steak and kidney pie, and the day it ran out of that he'd transfer his allegiance to another Italian restaurant. Bill, by the way, had a flat in Alassio and used the Hotel Europa and Continental there a lot. I went there once and found him the uncrowned king of Alassio. He knew the owner of the most important restaurant, which was a semi-night-club. There were very often friends of his there, like Max Bygraves, who used to do cabaret in this restaurant. Bill would sometimes get up and sing "I've Got a Loverly Bunch of Coconuts" for the British tourists there.

'As a result of working with Bill, I got to know quite a few of the cities of the United Kingdom, especially their music halls and railway stations. [Ronnie's agreement with Bill had allowed fortnightly shows so that Bill could continue touring the theatres on alternate weeks, then come in for a week's television rehearsal.] I would go up to York or Leeds or Cardiff or whatever by the morning train with ideas for the next show. In the afternoon we would go to the theatre to rehearse the boys in the stuff they hadn't seen before. On the train back I would map out the camera script, and since the journey back might take four or five hours I would arrive back at base with a rough script and continuity, plus what we had been able to work out with the boys in rehearsal.

'Of course, we had guest artists. They used to do their own spot and then a duet with Bill. Bill loved working with other people. My favourite guest artist show was when I had Dickie Henderson, Senior, with Bill Cotton and we put in Dickie Henderson and Bill Cotton, Juniors. Young Bill Cotton was then not even known in the BBC. He was still a music publisher with Johnny Johnson in Michael Reine Music. Jimmy Grafton wrote a very funny piece for the two fathers and the two sons, which ended with the four of them dancing to "Tip-Toe Through the Tulips" – the old Dick Henderson routine. That was a very warm occasion.

'There were always plenty of jokes. Some of them were standing jokes, like my university background. There was a day when I had to get my M.A. degree from Oxford. [Bill Cotton always said that Brian Tesler came from Cambridge. He was mistaken, but it was all an Oxford and Cambridge boat race to him.] After you've got your M.A. you go and dress yourself up in a gown and mortar-board and collect your degree officially from the university. The *Daily Express* got on to it, and telephoned Bill about his producer receiving an M.A. Bill told them, "Since both of us are so bleedin' cultured it shouldn't be surprising for my producer to be a Master of Arts, so I can't understand why the *Daily Express* is asking about it."

'In all the television Band Shows, Bill's personality came through entire. We always used to have a big production finale involving Bill. He worked terribly hard through the show, terribly hard, and I didn't know he had back trouble until one day I burst into his dressing room and found him naked on the floor being pummelled by a great big muscular fellow, who turned out to be his masseur.

'After the shows we would always go to the Empress, when Tommy Gale the restaurateur used to run it. Then, when everybody else had gone home, Bill would say, "Come on, let's go to the Astor. They might have an act there we could use in the show." So we would go across the road and we'd sit down and have a drink, and Bill would fall fast asleep, and I would watch the show. At the end of the show I would wake him up and we would go home. He had this great capacity for falling asleep. It was one of the things that kept him going. A man of that age and bulk, doing the things that he did – he had to have some way of resting up, so he cat-napped. He slept through more shows at the Astor than we'd had hot dinners beforehand.'

Bill and Max Bygraves impersonating the
Dolly Sisters.

Jimmy Grafton wrote the scripts for the TV
Band Shows for over eight years.

Jimmy Grafton, long the comedy writer and script man for the television Band Show, had a characteristically trying introduction to Billy Cotton.

'In the fifties, when I was shifting my scripting activities from radio to television, I was asked by Bill Ward of ATV if I would script a television Band Show for Billy Cotton. Up to this point I had never met Bill, although I had frequently listened to his radio show, and knew something about his earlier activities as a racing driver. I also knew that, like myself, he was born and bred in the City of Westminster, which I hoped would provide a link between us. I was warned, however, that Bill was a blunt, straightforward man who was continually on his guard against being patronized, and might not be too easy to get on good terms with immediately.

'As I subsequently discovered for myself, Bill was a man who treated all other men as equals. Although he bossed his own band, he never lorded it over them and was not prepared to kow-tow to others. He was particularly offended by people who put on airs or acted in what he used to describe as an "arsy-tarsy" manner. It was a little unfortunate, then, that when I was conducted into his presence at a band rehearsal a well-meaning individual introduced me as Major Jimmy Grafton and then, knowing of the possible common ground with Bill, added, "He's a Westminster City Councillor." Bill looked me up and down. "Oh, is he?" he said. "That must be nice for him." He then returned to his band to rehearse another number, leaving me to sit uncomfortably waiting for him to resume our conversation – if he ever intended to.

'At the end of the session Bill returned to me. Basically a compassionate man, he wanted to put me at my ease, not to say himself. "Westminster, eh?" he said. "Went to Westminster School, did you?" "No," I said, "I was at school in Kent, but I did go to Westminster City [the local secondary school] before that. Did you go there?" Bill laughed. "Me, mate? Not me. I was one of the ragged-arsed militia." Desperately I produced my trump card. "Well, anyway, if you were brought up in Westminster, you probably know my pub." That made Bill sit up a bit. "Pub?" he said. "What pub's that?" "Graftons," I told him. "It's been in our family since 1848." By now Bill was beaming. "Christ Almighty! I know your bleedin' pub. Many's the Sunday morning I've stood on the corner opposite, waiting for it to open."

'The next few minutes were spent in comparing notes on local personalities and shop-keepers, many then defunct. The question of scripting and any

115

anxiety he might have had as to whether I would be right for the job were forgotten. We were both Westminster lads and that was enough. Thus began a friendship which lasted until Bill's death.

'A short ATV series was followed by the longer BBC one under the guidance of my friend – and one of the finest ever light entertainment producers – Brian Tesler, who is now chief executive of London Weekend Television. Together with Brian, Bill, and Bill's friend the choreographer Leslie Roberts, the Billy Cotton Television Band Show was put together, and I continued to write it for eight years until it was changed to a variety format. During this time Michael Hurll, now one of the busiest light entertainment producers, rose from call boy on the show to assistant floor manager, then to floor manager, and finally to producer of the programme.

'Writing comedy numbers for the band was something I always enjoyed. There were some natural characters among them. Particularly Bill Herbert, the oldest member of the band, Laurie Johnson, little Frankie Kenyon, and of course Alan Breeze. Breezy was an almost inarticulate stutterer, but could sing fast Cockney songs with complete fluency. I suggested that conversations with Breezy would be easier if he sang instead of spoke. "Don't tell him that for Gawd's sake," said Bill. "I get enough of his lip anyway. I don't want it to music."

'Bill was fond of his band, and counted them all as his friends, but this didn't stop him from being a thorough martinet when he wanted to be. Rehearsals, especially with the comedy numbers, where members of the band had acting-singing roles, usually in some unlikely garb, were often the scene of some choice language from Bill, but were usually good fun. To see old Bill Herbert dressed as William Tell's son with an apple on his head, or the whole motley crew in a skit on the Scarlet Pimpernel sung to the Boccherini minuet, was as much of a laugh for the participants as it was for the audience. Bill himself either participated in skits or appeared in occasional cut-away camera shots with a look of stoically endured suffering or a spontaneous convulsion of mirth. Another task I enjoyed was writing duets for Bill and Russ Conway, the handsome, smiling pianist-composer who made his name on the show. Russ was basically a shy man, but he had a great rapport with Billy and enjoyed the twitting of one another that was part of the act. Theirs was a very successful relationship, and I know Russ feels he owes a great deal to Bill.

'Another successful introduction into the show was Jeremy Lloyd, as a chinless wonder or upper-class twit, complete with bowler hat and umbrella, providing a great foil to Bill's blunt Cockney attitude, and always ready

Rehearsing a comedy routine: Laurie Johnson,
Frankie Kenyon, Alan Breeze, Bill Herbert, and
Billy Cotton.

to con Bill into some idiotic scheme for the show which usually ended in his discomfiture. A typical example was Jeremy's return to the show broke after his holiday, in a packing case marked COD, which Bill had to pay for, and which contained not only Jeremy but a girl friend. Jeremy is, of course, more active these days as a much sought after script writer, but he continually meets people who still remember his appearances on the Billy Cotton Band Show. At the beginning, he met the same defensively aloof and sardonic attitude from Bill that greeted anyone who could be suspected of being toffee-nosed or patronizing. Jeremy, the last person in the world to be either of those things, had his own difficulties in communicating with Bill, who insisted on calling him Jerry and categorizing him in characteristic fashion as "arsy-tarsy". The breakthrough, almost literally, came during a show which also featured the wrestler and stunt man Doug Robinson, with whom Jeremy had to undertake some comic judo and be thrown. The result was a couple of cracked ribs, but also some definitely broken ice, and "Jerry" found Bill regarding him with a new respect.

'One always had to earn Bill's friendship, but once it was given it was there for good. He was, too, the most generous performer, in that his guests on the show were always given the best possible presentation. He was happy to work with them if he could, but always conscious of his own shortcomings as a memorizer of scripts or reader of lines. The teleprompter, or "autocue", that revolves beneath the camera to be read line by line by those who distrust their memories, was the bane of his life – a troublesome necessity that elicited some very odd phrasing from time to time as Bill ploughed gallantly on, occasionally missing out punctuation or pausing in mid-sentence. Such minor slips were of no account to his vast army of fans, who found him only more lovable because of them.

'Bill always managed to be right on the ball when singing on his own, joining in a comedy number, or sharing a duet with Kathie Kay or guests such as Alma Cogan and even Jayne Mansfield. A sentimental man at heart, he enjoyed sentimental songs. He also had a great sense of fun whenever he allowed himself to show it, and with his Cockney dislike of frills he was always ready to cut any situation down to size. Once we went to Paris to record a programme from the Nouvelle Eve Night Club. Tonia Bern (later to marry Donald Campbell) and the beautiful dancer Aleta Morrison were both in the show, and joined Bill, Bill Junior, and myself for a meal afterwards at a Hungarian restaurant. Here we were regaled by a bevy of French violinists in traditional gipsy garb playing zigeuner music. Bill solemnly beckoned over the maître d'hôtel and asked, "Can they play requests,

Jeremy Lloyd played an upper-class foil to Bill's Cockney.

mate?" "Of course, Monsieur." "Will you ask them to play 'Maybe It's Because I'm a Londoner'?"

'When the "Wakey-Wakey Tavern" was instituted, paid extras were used as background customers, but occasionally friends of the cast were included – out of camera-shot if possible. My daughter Sally, then thirteen, was a keen fan of the show, and was thrilled when Brian Tesler allowed her to look around the set. Brian wasn't so pleased when one of his cameras picked up a thirteen-year-old unpaid extra ostensibly drinking in the tavern. A quicker cutaway was never made!

'Bill's appeal to young people as well as old was based not only on his breezy personality and straightforward approach, but also, I believe, on audiences' instinctive recognition of his underlying kindness and honesty. Like most people in show business, he was occasionally beset by the anxieties and insecurities of the profession, but he was held in esteem and respect by his fellow professionals, and with affection by all. The greatest legacy a man can leave is that he lives in the minds and hearts of his friends and those who loved him. I am proud to count myself among them.'

WHAT BILL COTTON TAUGHT MICHAEL HURLL

Michael Hurll began by looking after the props in the show, and went on to become Bill's last television producer.

'Bill was a pretty imposing character, larger than life, with a very bluff exterior but a heart of gold. If you ever had a row with him he usually made it up the next day by buying you the biggest meal in the world. He could have tremendous rows. He'd have these shout-ups with me, slam the door and leave, and next minute he'd come back inside and make it all up again. He had supreme self-confidence. He had the ability to walk on a stage as if the audience was very lucky to be watching him, and that, I think, is the hallmark of any great star.

'Bill couldn't read music, and yet he had the acclaim of the highest professionals. David McCallum, the leader of the London Philharmonic, sometimes used to sit in when we were augmenting the violins, and he put Bill Cotton amongst the three top conductors in the world: Malcolm Sargent, John Barbirolli, and then Bill Cotton. He said they were the three who could get what they wanted out of the orchestra, could communicate with the musicians and get the best possible performance from them. Bill used to defend his musicians humorously by saying that hungry bandsmen made the best musicians as far as he was concerned. And they were most loyal and hard-working for him, though one or two of them never opened their instrument cases between one show and the next. If you haven't played a clarinet for a fortnight the reed becomes brittle and you get terrible squeaks and noises. Bill used to say his woodwind had not got reeds in them·but floorboards.

'It would have been very easy to criticize Bill, but he was far too nice a man to criticize, and he was too lovable as far as the public were concerned. You felt you were rotten if you criticized him. But he could defend himself by enormous exaggeration; I used to tell him that he was an incredible liar. I remember he had done an under-par show one Saturday and he knew it, and he went home for Sunday to his flat in Bury Street, St. James's. It was freezing cold that weekend, and snow fell all through the Sunday. On the Monday morning he telephoned me, and I remarked, "Well, Bill, it wasn't too good on Saturday night, was it?" He said, "Well, yesterday as I was walking down the street people were coming up to me left,right and centre, saying what a wonderful show it was." "You liar!" I said. "There wasn't a soul out in the centre of London yesterday. There are pictures in the paper to prove it – London deserted, snow a foot deep, and not a soul about. Nobody came up to you, and if they were out they wouldn't have stopped to congratulate you."

'It amused me that he lived in St. James's, because whenever he used to say, "I'm just going to pop round to the grocer's," he meant Fortnum and Mason's. That was the only store around, and he used to treat it as the corner shop. And it was amazing, if you ever did go into "the grocer's" with him, because bowler-hatted retired Army colonels were always tipping their hats to him, saying, "Good morning" and passing the time of day in Sandhurst accents. Bill, of course, had a tremendous command of his own version of the English language, especially when he let fly. I was driving in a car with him through Soho, and some taxi-driver cut him up. He gave this taxi-driver a mouthful out of the window. There were some real rough down-and-outs opposite the back entrance of where Lyons used to be, and they were so impressed by this language that they all tipped their hats to him.

'He admired artists like Cilla Black, Russ Conway, and Max Bygraves, who worked a lot with Bill in the stage shows and was a regular guest on our show. I think Bill was better working with young people. Naturally I was very pleased when I became his producer, because it meant that Bill had confidence in me – and I had started off seven years earlier at the age of nineteen just pushing the props on in his shows. I produced some twenty-five over the last three years. Bill taught me an awful lot about show business and about dealing with personalities, but he was a very tough person to work with. He was very good at what we call the "running order", the building of a sequence in a variety show. You have to have a good opening number, and then you might think you can settle for a bit, but he used to say that the third item is very important. If you haven't got something good as the third item, that is the moment people decide whether they are going to stay with you or switch over.

'I miss him most because to me it wasn't just a person but a way of life that disappeared. He was a part of my life. I remember now how he used to refer to people as "silly sods", and I really think he looks down from Heaven every now and then, and whenever I make a terrible mistake on a programme I can hear him saying, "You silly sod, haven't I warned you about that, and you have gone and done it again!"'

COTTON AND SON

Preceding Michael Hurll as producer of the Band Show was Bill's son, Bill Cotton, Junior, winning his spurs for the BBC. 'He made a terrific job of it,' declares veteran Bill Herbert. 'He made the show so successful – he had the old man's ability for knowing what the public wants. Old Bill and young Bill used to sit in the front, and we'd go through the numbers, and as often as not it was young Bill who would come right in and say, "I don't like that bit, we want to bring the other bit in instead, but otherwise it seems all right." Then we'd change these spots, and generally we did it right. Young Bill had that ability as a producer – of course, he was on the Palladium staff for a long time. Anyway, when they gave him the chance to produce our show he did it with terrific success, and of course took it into the Royal Command Performances.'

Bill Senior once said, 'I can never adequately express my appreciation of the loyalty, love, and service of my son Bill Junior. It was a moving moment when he was asked to propose my health at a dinner of the Anglo-American Sporting Club. Young Bill got up and said what, perhaps understandably among us reticent Cottons, he had never said before. He said that he was realizing a great ambition in being able for the first time to pay public tribute to a father whom he described as "a man's man, with the ability to join the ladies". He said my life had spanned the halcyon days of the big band, and continued beyond that time, surviving by "blind faith and courage and the ability to take life by the scruff of the neck and make it do what he wanted it to". Thanks, Bill!'

Bill Cotton with Bill Senior. A great team.

Rita Williams (centre) with members of the High-Lights and the band in a number called 'Don't Do It, Nelly' from the TV series of 1963.

Billy Cotton's band always had a reputation for comedy. The most memorable number must be 'I've Got a Loverly Bunch of Coconuts' – certainly the Queen Mother, who was no mean shot with the coconuts at the Command Performance, and Her Majesty the Queen herself, who 'copped it' rather unfortunately on her tiara at Christmastime, must have their private memories of this song. 'The original idea for the ending of the number was Ray Landis's,' said Bill. 'I was looking for some way to close the piece, and Ray asked if it was any good throwing featherweights, as they sometimes used to do then at carnival dances. I told him it was a rotten idea. A few weeks later I thought of it myself – at least, I thought I had thought of it – and we put it in the show. Since then I have tried all sorts of fancy production gimmicks, but audiences never welcomed anything like the "snowball throwballs".'

Ray Landis got caught out himself once. Billy never used music-stands for the band, expecting them to know the programme by heart. He also expected them to know the little secret signs he used, for example to announce a cut of a few bars when the show was over-running in time. 'Ray Landis joined in the last year of the war,' Bill said. 'He came straight into the band at Bournemouth, and he was given no rehearsal, just a quick run-through, with some of the boys clueing him up. He was an experienced trumpeter, and although for the first show he had no music, he wrote out all the hints that the boys had given him on a little card and hid it all over the place. The last number in that show was Breezy singing "Ashby de la Zouch" followed by some sort of sea song, at the end of which Frankie Kenyon, dressed as a sailor, jumped into the arms of Phil Phillips, also in naval rig, and the whole band marched out playing "Anchors Aweigh". But I signalled for a cut, and they had forgotten to tell Ray Landis about the signals. The whole band marched smartly off except for Ray, who was left playing his nautical march on his tod.'

LOVABLE RITA WILLIAMS

Rita Williams joined as head of Cotton's singing group, in its various disguises, in 1951. The *Radio Times* once described her as 'a beauty with brown hair and green eyes. Four-feet-eleven, with the darting energy of a squirrel and the quick-change artistry of a chameleon. She can play Madame Maigret, a schoolgirl, and Helen Shapiro in a single programme, and still have breath to sing mezzo, contralto or soprano.'

Charles Young, of the High-Lights, remembers the great support that came from life with Rita. 'As a person you could not fault her on professionalism. She really was the epitome of a pro. Anyone who booked singers from her would be sure to get exactly what they wanted, and always on time. She would step in at the last moment for anyone who didn't appear. We were recording with Donald Peers and he came to the session without knowing the song. She sang it to him, actually taught it to him, before the session started. She was the perfection of reliability. And the comedy came naturally to her. With an awful lot of the parts that were written for her, like "Mrs Spiegel", a lot of her own personality went into it. And whenever there was the sort of stage accident which makes you dissolve in laughter – a thing which seemed to happen quite often on the Cotton Show – she would weigh in to try and pull us out of it.

'Once at the Shepherds Bush Theatre Alan Breeze was on stage singing a "lonely range" number, a real slow cowboy song, and we had to do a lot of "hoo, ahoo, ahoos" offstage as backing. Then over on the other side of the stage we suddenly saw Barney Gilbraith in costume for the next sketch, which we had not previously seen. He was wearing a fez, a striped football shirt, long socks, and a pair of boots – all of which made him look like a cut-off Tommy Cooper. But in addition to that he was carrying a rolled umbrella and a miner's lamp. We were setting eyes on him for the first time in this get-up, and it was more than we could take. You can imagine having to sing "hoo, ahoo" for a cowboy song and someone like that comes along and dries you up completely. Well, the "hoo, ahoos" started getting wobbly with our laughter, and the more you try to sing when you're laughing the worse it gets. I reckon I was the first to drop out. I tried to gain control and went back to "hoo, ahoo" and then the other fellows dropped out with the giggles. But there was Rita, digging me in the ribs with her elbow, trying to keep the show going, and saying, "Come on, Charlie, hoo, ahoo. Come on, Charlie, hoo ahoo." But I couldn't make it, and even she dried up in the end, so the whole backing collapsed. But it was Rita who tried to the last to keep us going.'

'I could always dry up that group if I wanted to,' Billy Cotton confessed with a chuckle. 'There was a song called "The Yawn Song", and it only needed me to start yawning somewhat extravagantly in front of them for them to find it quite impossible to sing.'

RUSS CONWAY

Russ Conway, of course, is one of Billy Cotton's most famous and successful discoveries. It was in October 1958 that a very nervous young composer and accompanist joined the show as resident honky-tonk piano player, and although he had already had a good deal of experience in show business, he could hardly have expected to achieve so quickly the popularity and fame that followed in the next few months. His records were all hits. His smile and personality made even Billy Cotton give way when the Silhouettes expressed an eagerness to help Mr Conway get his piano on or off the stage.

'There was an affinity between Billy Cotton and myself that even now I find very hard to explain,' says Russ. 'Except to say that I was extremely fond of him as a man, and will always be grateful for the opportunity of working with him and being able to study his professionalism; and in a humble way I hope some of it brushed off on me.

'One of the strange things about the Billy Cotton Shows was that I never actually played a honky-tonk piano on any of the television programmes. [A honky-tonk, or jangle-box piano, has specially treated strings.] But the mere fact of having the front taken out of the upright piano gave the impression that it was a honky-tonk instrument, and when playing an upright piano I invariably employ a more "tinkly" style of playing than I would on a concert grand. It was on the upright piano on the Billy Cotton Shows that I launched "Roulette", "China Tea", "Slowcoach", and "Royal Event", and I am quite sure that the fact that I was with Billy Cotton played a major part in the success of these tunes.

'Bill Cotton, Junior, when he was the producer of the show, was a tremendous help in calming one's nerves, and, believe me, we all get nerves on television. Young Bill would never say, "Smile on the sixteenth or thirty-second bar," but he would watch his TV monitors carefully, and when he saw a smile coming naturally, he would zoom in on a close-up. Unfortunately, as soon as I notice the camera is on me I tend to freeze a little, but here again Bill would cut the close-up and return to the keyboard or another angle. That in itself was a tremendous help to me.

'In my very early days with the show Rita Williams and her singers would often be leaning over the piano. Many times I'd have forgotten the chord construction of a tune through being nervous, but Rita would have written it down on a piece of paper which she would hold up outside the vision of the camera, and she and her singers would be watching to see whether I could actually read the notes she had in her hand. Of course, I used to fall apart at all this. Everything about the show was spontaneous, with people like Rita, Alan Breeze, Kathie Kay, Grisha Farfel, the Silhouettes and all the regulars. It was complete team work from the word "go", and in the

127

days when we were doing one show a week and transmitting it live, it was nothing out of the ordinary after the final rehearsal for us all to get together and see how much music we could cut to get the show on and off the air in the allotted time, and this could not have been done without the team work that existed within the permanent company.

'I shall forever be grateful for the experience I gained by working with such professionals.'

Bill Cotton always pointed to Russ Conway's success as an example of the unpredictable luck that sometimes rules show business. 'Bill Junior had heard him play in an agent's office, and he booked him to appear on "6.5 Special", which was one of the shows of the moment. He went down disastrously, for at that time the public were not looking for that sort of music. But Bill remembered him, and there came the time when he decided there ought to be a piano spot in the Billy Cotton Show. He booked young Russ, but, for his own protection, he put him on one of those rigorous contracts which write in options almost after the first five minutes, in case Russ still wasn't going down with the public. But, as fortune would have it, the moment he started with me coincided with his first real success with the record "Side Saddle", and the combination of the two was a snowball.'

KATHIE KAY SEES ACTION

Bill Junior was also responsible for introducing Kathie Kay to the Billy Cotton band set-up. 'Over the Christmas of 1956–7,' Bill Senior narrated, 'I had a six-week engagement at the Prince of Wales Theatre in London. Doreen Stephens, my vocalist, went sick, and I had to have a replacement for the last week. My son Bill then had a music publishing business in partnership with Johnny Johnson. Bill mentioned to Johnny that I needed a singer, and he suggested Kathie Kay, who was broadcasting regularly then with Peter Yorke and his Concert Orchestra in a show in which Johnny and the Johnson Brothers also had a spot. Kathie joined us for the last week, and from there she graduated to my regular radio and television shows.

'Kathie had a remarkable career. She went on the stage at the age of four, and before she was fourteen she had appeared in every London variety theatre, including the London Palladium. Later she married Archie McCulloch, the Glasgow impresario and journalist, had three sons, and made their welfare the centre of her life as long as they were young. She continued to do a certain amount of recording, and one day a record of hers was sticking out of her husband's brief-case when he called on a friend at the BBC. The friend insisted on playing it, and it was on the turntable when the head of

128

Billy Cotton and Kathie Kay.

Alma Cogan was one of Bill's favourite guest stars.

variety walked in. He said, "I like what I hear; I want that girl," and Kathie began a second singing career in broadcasting, television, and recording: not full-time, for she refused to make her home in London, and still ranked her boys as her primary concern. She notched well over a million miles in flights between Glasgow and London alone. When she first joined my band I agreed that because her sons were still young she should not travel around to theatre engagements with the band, but should confine herself to broadcasting and records. We made a charity record together, of a tune called "Five Pennies" with the words re-written to suit the old folks, and we collected more than a thousand pounds with it one Christmas. I thought our voices blended so well together that I persuaded my recording manager, Norman Newell of Columbia, and Kathie's, Wally Ridley of HMV, to set up a long-playing disc, and we made the very successful "Bill and Kate".'

Kathie Kay and Rita Williams were, with Alan Breeze, the singers in the 'Wakey-Wakey Tavern' show in the Royal Command Variety Performance of 1960. Max Bygraves and Russ Conway were guests in the tavern, and the High-Lights were the regulars Barney Gilbraith, Charles Young, Charles Granville, and John McCarthy. In the band, Jack Branston had replaced Wilbur Jones on sax. The trumpet line was the same. Harry Buckles replaced Alfie Reece on trombone. Joe Hodson was on drums, and Jock Reid came in on sousaphone and Archie Slavin on second guitar. At the piano, where Clem Bernard had reigned so long, sat George McCallum.

ALMA COGAN, PARTY GIRL

'Alma Cogan was always one of my favourite guest stars,' said Bill Cotton. 'We got on like a house on fire, and she would turn up at any time to appear in a last-minute spot with me. We used to sit up in her flat, working out the routines. I was very fond of her.'

Kathie Kay remembers Alma's flat because of the parties she used to hold there. 'Alma was one of Bill's favourite artists because she had an awful lot of fun in her. She used to play practical jokes on him, and vice versa, so when we knew she was coming on the show it was fun. One time we were all invited to a party in her Kensington flat, where she lived with her mother and sister. We all had to dress up as Australians. When we got to the flat, which was gorgeous normally, all the furniture had been taken out of the lounge, the drapes were down, and here we were with great ugly old trestles and coarse plates and mugs with our names on, and everybody had to talk Australian. But that was Alma. If she went to any part of the world she came back and had a party.'

Jayne Mansfield's appearance on the show was
memorable in more ways than one!

Kathie remembers when they had Jayne Mansfield on the show. 'It was very difficult to get artists to fit in with our programme schedule. She was filming, and staying at Paddy Roberts's house near the studio, so Bill had to go out there a couple of times and rehearse the songs they were going to do. On the night before the show she had to come to Shepherds Bush for camera and sound line-ups. She was late, but she finally arrived wearing a white ermine coat. She was full of apologies, and she said, "I've got nothing on. I've just slipped on my fur coat and dashed here." The rehearsal started, and we were all sitting in the audience watching. She had a number with Bill where they finished with a little dance at the end, and he had to pass her in front of him with a sort of twirl-around and she had a curtsey at the end of it. Well, as she twirled round in front of Bill, the fur coat flew open, and we all – particularly the cameraman – saw that she was speaking the bare truth when she said, "I've got nothing on." At the end of her act Bill Herbert came forward sheepishly with a bit of paper and looked at her adoringly, but said nothing. "Autograph?" she asked brightly. "No," he whispered. "Telephone number!"'

BOB HOPE MEETS THE GUV'NOR

Bob Hope also appeared on the Billy Cotton Band Show. 'The fact is,' said Bill, 'I didn't ask him; his agent asked the BBC if he could appear. And he had to be content with the little money that was left in the till for that programme.'

Michael Hurll was watching, and describes Bob Hope's entry for rehearsal. 'A party met Bob Hope at the door, but Bill Cotton just sat in the stalls watching, and let Bob Hope get on stage, get made up, sit on stage, and then rehearse. Finally he said, "Right. We like that. We'll record it. I'll just go and change now and put on my make-up. And Bob Hope was left sitting on stage for about twenty minutes waiting for Bill Cotton.'

Bill Cotton later commented, 'One or two of Bob's entourage seemed to think I was handing him the frozen mitt, and Bob himself seemed a little worried for a time. Then I saw him say something to Bill Junior, and the atmosphere seemed to clear and the show went on all right. After the show I had more time for Bob and we became great buddies. Later I asked my son what Bob had said to him at the end of their consultation, and he told me that Bob had said, "We have a saying in America, 'Never argue with City Hall!'" I was glad to see this acceptance of "We'll play it the Guv'nor's way". As far as I, the Guv'nor, was concerned, I had a show to get away and a good guest star in it. But there had been scores of shows before and would be scores afterwards. If I let a rehearsal be put out of joint by paying too much public attention to a visiting fireman, then the present show would be bound to suffer. And that wasn't my idea at all.'

FROM NORTH OF THE BORDER: LARRY MARSHALL

Larry Marshall, Scotland's most accomplished and inventive comedian, has fond memories of the time he was asked to appear on the Band Show. He was starring in 'The 1 O'Clock Gang', then Scottish Television's programme with the highest ratings, which went out at lunch-time five days a week, Monday to Friday, for over eight years and became something of a family institution.

Bill was in Glasgow for a few days, staying with Kathie Kay and her husband. He had heard so much about 'The 1 O'Clock Gang' that he decided he must watch it. He immediately recognized Larry Marshall's great talent and decided there and then that he would invite Larry to guest on a forthcoming Band Show.

Larry recalls: 'Bill was on the phone to me within minutes of the show ending. I was in my dressing room when someone shouted, "There's Billy Cotton on the line for you." I thought, Billy *Cotton*? Mmmm, either they had the name wrong or it was someone else with the same name. I did not think it could be *the* Billy Cotton! I was immediately won over by Bill – he spoke to me in such glowing and appreciative terms that I don't think my feet touched the ground for the rest of the month. Bill's relaxed and warm manner made me feel as though we were old friends. I agreed to come down to London at the end of the month and appear on the Band Show. I considered it the very greatest of honours.

'I did a sketch for Bill on the show, and in the run-throughs and rehearsals I think I must have learnt more than in the preceding ten years. Bill had an uncanny ear for the delivery of lines and an uncanny sense of timing. He was continually inventive and could breathe life into the most hackneyed routines. We did what was known as the "Bus Stop" sketch: I was standing in the street with my hand on a bus stop. People gradually began forming behind me until there was a sizeable queue. Then the queue began murmuring, "Where's the bus then, Jimmy?" and, "Is this service no longer operating, then?" And eventually I said, "You'll not get a bus here. The stop's around the corner. I'm only standing here waiting for the Ministry of Works van to take me and the temporary stop away."'

Larry Marshall, who unexpectedly 'treated' Bill to a meal!

Larry remembers that after the TV show Bill invited him to come back the next Sunday for the radio broadcast and to join him and a few others for lunch after the show.

'Bill drove us from the Aeolian Hall in New Bond Street to a very grand restaurant in Soho. As Bill walked into this restaurant the waiters and the manager seemed to drop everything and make straight for him. They made a tremendous fuss of him and then seated us in Bill's favourite corner. Nothing was too much trouble for the staff and we had a superb meal with plenty to drink. Yet, for some reason, when the bill was presented, Bill wasn't to be seen. One moment he was there, the next he had disappeared! I could not understand it. So the bill was given to me. I gingerly picked it up from the plate and turned it slowly – £50! A lot of money in those days for anyone! But for a Scotsman – it was a prince's fortune! I realized I had no option but to pay up. And I did. Whenever I met Bill after this he would mention the meal and say how touched he was that one of Scotland's sons had treated him to such a fine meal. And I would always say that I considered it an honour. It *was* an honour and, needless to say, Bill subsequently treated me to a few grand meals too!'

Larry Marshall regrets that he did not work with Bill on more occasions. But he thanks Fate that he did have at least one opportunity to do so. And that occasion he will never forget.

FRANKIE VAUGHAN

Frankie Vaughan was a guest on the television Band Show, but he had met Billy Cotton long before that.

'I wasn't even in show business when I first met Billy Cotton. I had qualified at the Leeds College of Art, and was still there – as a student teacher. I had to make up my mind where I was going from there: whether I should continue as a teacher or branch out into something like commercial or industrial art.

'I had been singing with local bands in and around Leeds, and the man who was keeping a fatherly eye on me and looking for ways of launching me as a professional singer was BBC producer Barney Colehan. We heard that Billy might be looking for a singer for his stage band show, so I went to Nottingham to see him – and he was so kind and considerate.

'He told me that, yes, he might well be looking for a singer. Then he asked me, "Do you really want to go into show business?" As a matter of fact, I didn't want to go into show business. I wasn't too keen on the idea at all. I suppose I was really in two minds about it. "Once you feel you

Frankie Vaughan well remembers Bill's consideration.

know what you want to do," said Billy, "come back and see me again." Which was fair enough.

'Years later, when I was well and truly in show business, I had the great thrill of guesting on his television show. It was THE family show of the time – and THE show to be on. Me, I was very, very nervous.

'I reminded Billy where we had first met. "Well," he said, "you've obviously made up your mind now!" And he congratulated me.

'I remember particularly the rehearsals for that show. The band rehearsal was very thorough. Billy kept saying to me, "Is that all right, son?" and, "We'll do it until you're happy with it." I had never been shown such consideration before.

'But the thing that amazed me was the way he personally waltzed through the rehearsals. He had a marvellous, casual manner about him – as though it was all just a bit of fun. I couldn't quite understand it. It was only years later that I realized he was saving everything up for the show itself.

'He knew, of course, that I was very nervous. And so just before the show began he walked into my dressing room with a glass of wine in his hand. I didn't drink very much in those days, but he said to me, "Here's a glass of plonk, son – get that bleedin' lot down you and you'll be great!" He gave me a laugh, and I went on and did the show and it was a tremendous experience.

'I think this was when I really appreciated the wonderful rapport he had with the audience – who forgave him every little mistake he made. And he'd look at me and give me a wink as though to say, "We're all quite normal and we make mistakes, so get on with it and don't worry." He had the extraordinary ability of showing that a mistake was quite normal. And if he made a mistake, he did it broadly. He wasn't ashamed of it. It was a lesson I've never forgotten.'

SANDIE SHAW FINDS A SHOULDER

Bill would always go out of his way to give a nervous youngster confidence. 'The show demanded that, too,' he said. 'I had Sandie Shaw on my show once in her early days. We were to sing the duet "Oh, Yes, I Remember It Well" from *Gigi*. The poor kid was very plainly nervous. Nothing was going right. So I stopped the rehearsal and took young Sandie aside, and I said, "Come here, Sandie. Forget this is a big show. Just pretend I'm your father. I'm old enough to be your grand-father, anyway. Come over here and put your head on my shoulder, and we'll try again." And that is how we played the scene for the duet, and Sandie knew very thankfully that it had gone very well.'

CILLA SANG TO HER MUM

Bill gave the same support to Cilla Black on her first show with him. 'She was very nervous,' he remembered. 'But before the show she had told me how fond her mother was of me. "Sing to your Mum," I told her. "*I will* – I always sing first to the mothers." And everything was all right.'

'It's quite true,' says Cilla. 'My Mum always fancied Bill, he was really her favourite. I felt I had always known Bill, because I remembered him from when I was a kid as being part of Sunday lunch-time with the radio. I really lived with Bill Cotton, he went with the roast beef and roast potatoes. In fact, I can smell the Sunday lunch when I think of him. After he found out he was my Mum's favourite he always remembered her. Once he actually sent her a message over the television and she almost passed out. We had just done a number together one Saturday night, and we were chatting afterwards. Then he sent his love to my mother, and she was watching, and she nearly fainted.

'The great thing with Billy was that he loved working with young people. I flew into town for dinner with him one night, and we went to a restaurant in Sloane Street. I had never been anywhere so posh. But Bill insisted on ordering all my food. "Oh, you'll like this," he'd say, and I usually did enjoy what he ordered. But he really was like an Angel Gabriel when I worked with him. He was always wanting to give me a cup of tea and feeding me up, because I was always very thin.

'It was a great thrill for me to do the Billy Cotton Band Show, because I remembered it from seeing it before I was a professional, when Russ Conway was the idol, the dreamboat, and everybody had to watch on Saturday night for Russ Conway. And Kathie Kay was great to me, always nice. When I was up in Scotland I met her husband, who I think worked on the *Express* at the time. I remember saying to him, "Well, thank God I was nice to your wife!"

'It was just like one big happy family, really, that was the atmosphere I felt. I was made very welcome. Bill was great. We were once doing a song called "If the Young Ones Are Happy, Then the Old Ones Should Be Glad". I didn't know it all that well, but Bill had recorded it and knew it quite well. We had to do a little dance. At that time I wasn't very good at the soft-shoe shuffle, so I said to him, "Gosh, I wish I could do that again." I didn't mean him to do anything about it, but he stopped all the action.

Cilla Black – 'The Girl' sang to her Mum.
BBC COPYRIGHT

He stopped everything and he called out to Michael Hurll, "Oi! Young man!" (he never called him Michael). "The Girl wants to do it again." (That's what he always called me, "The Girl".) And we did it again, even though we didn't really have the time. He was a soft sort of person, but in a way kind of hard – I suppose just a typical Cockney. What appealed to me was that I came from the same background – sort of rough and ready – and that is what I liked about Bill.'

Everyone liked Bill's rough and ready manner. 'Bill Junior once booked Vanessa Lee,' Bill recalled. 'I had only heard of her as an Ivor Novello type, and I grumbled about what I should be expected to do with her. Young Bill said, "She's marvellous. I'm sure you will get on with her." The moment Vanessa Lee saw me in the studio she walked up to me and she said, "I understand you're a right old bastard!" Well, that was a marvellous introduction, and from that time we got on famously. Bill Junior used to say he got quite bored with the way whenever there was a blank in the show I used to ask, "Why don't we get Vanessa Lee back?"'

MIKE HAWTHORN'S BUGLE CALL

When Mike Hawthorn was world motor-racing champion, Bill asked him to come on the show in the 'Wakey-Wakey Tavern' sketch. They devised a set-up which started with Bill sitting at one of the tables shooting a line about motor-racing. A dour character in one corner kept glumly questioning what he was saying, and finally asked, 'Why don't you stick to band leading!' This was Mike Hawthorn. Mike had been at the same school as Bill's two sons, Ted and Bill, Ardingly College in Sussex. He had been in the school band as a bugler – and Bill had, in fact, presented the college band with its instruments. At the end of the turn Mike Hawthorn played a bugle call from his old days. Only a few days later he announced his retirement from motor-racing, but within two months he was tragically killed in a road accident in Surrey.

Bill made another sentimental and generous gesture to the juvenile band of his youth when in 1967 he led his own 1st Westminster Troop of the Boy Scouts into the Ralph Reader Gang Show inside his own Band Show.

DISASTERS

Bill Cotton asked Peter Sellers on to his show, but the result was a comic form of disaster. 'Peter is renowned as an ad-libber,' Bill explained. 'What-

The exploding piano ...

... and what was left afterwards!

ever the words of the script started out to be, he manages to embroider them and often adds to them. Whereas I, not so nimble, stick to my script and rely heavily on the teleprompter to remind me where I am. However, whatever cue-lines I expected to get from Peter certainly did not come my way as he jazzed up the script. The viewers may have thought that I was staring with fixed and worried gloom at the camera, but I was really glaring with despair at the teleprompter, trying to make up my mind where we were!'

Bill remembered another time when things had gone wrong. 'Sometimes the BBC used to film material for future shows while we were fulfilling touring engagements. I was doing a summer season in Jersey, and a unit came over to film a sequence for the next series. Alan Breeze was supposed to sit down at the piano, which would immediately collapse into matchwood. This was to be done by putting a small amount of explosive inside the dummy piano. Unfortunately somebody had wrongly estimated the explosive charge. There was an enormous roar. The piano went up like a bomb, and lamentably some of the BBC team were badly hurt. I did not know immediately how serious it was, and I thought the best thing was to carry on with a gag. "It must have been something I ate!" I said.'

THE FANTASTIC MRS MILLS

Mrs Mills was on the bill during that Jersey summer season. She was another artist who made a meteoric rise to fame greatly helped by the Billy Cotton Band Show. In the autumn of 1961 she was working as the superintendent of a typing pool at the London office of the Paymaster-General. For fun she sometimes played the piano with a group of friends at local club functions near her home in Loughton, Essex. One Saturday night she was spotted by a theatrical agent and was asked to make a record. It sold sixty thousand copies and reached the Top Twenty. She was put into the Billy Cotton Band Show in early December, and again on Christmas Eve, and finished that month playing at Buckingham Palace with top-line variety acts giving a charity show. She was signed up to appear in every Billy Cotton Band Show in the next series. 'Goodness,' she said. 'It's unbelievable. Quite fantastic!'

'Bill Cotton was marvellous,' says Mrs Mills, recalling their first meeting. 'I was taken to the TV Centre to meet Bill Cotton, Junior, and Bill Senior walked in as young Bill was playing a record that my recording manager, Norman Newell, had got me to do. He said "Hello" to me and I said "Hello" to him, though I didn't know him from Adam, and he said to young Bill, "Who's that, then?" Young Bill said, "It's 'er." Old Bill said, "She hasn't got many problems, by the looks of her tum, has she?" I was trembling

Mrs Mills owes much of her success to her
appearances on the show.

Russ Conway, Alma Cogan, Billy Cotton,
Norman Newell, and Bill Junior before the
recording session for the record that we include.

at the knees, but he said, "It's nice to meet you," and he shook hands, and Kathie shook hands, and I sat down and they talked to me about going on the show. I eventually did seven months straight off.

'We used to have lots of fun on the show. I remember doing a medley of Fats Waller tunes, including "My Very Good Friend the Milkman". Bill went into the wardrobe and brought out two pints and put them on the stage by me. This was on the actual show and I didn't know it was going to happen, and I just fell about almost in hysterics.

'He was having a go at the boys one day – the more he went on at them the more he got out of them, and they respected him greatly. I walked on to the set – they were rehearsing something – and I said to the boys, "Hello, lads, has old Thunderguts been at you again?" Bill said, "I'll give you Thunderguts!" But after that I used to call him that for devilment, in the nicest possible way, affectionately.

'I used to admire the way it didn't matter to him who was coming on the stage, he always put them at their ease right away. He had that something about him.'

'I don't think it was possible not to love him,' says Norman Newell, who was also Bill's recording manager. 'He was cantankerous, of course, at times, but not to me. He used to live quite near me in the country, and it was one of his delights when I would phone him and say, "Steak and kidney pudding!" He would be over like a shot. But I did perceive a loneliness in Bill Cotton. I always thought he was a very lonely man. But his jokes were fantastic. Once when Tony Lewis was ill in bed with flu, Bill asked an undertaker to call. Tony took it all right. He said, "Would you drive round the block a few more times, and I might be gone." '

A TYPICAL EPISODE

Billy Cotton's way with the band is shown in this episode involving the veteran trumpeter Grisha Farfel.

Once during rehearsal the band couldn't get one Latin American number right, and finally, in despair, Bill said, 'We'll forget it.'

At that point a little voice with an accent came from the back. 'Bill, I think I know what's wrong with the number.'

Bill pushed his glasses up on his forehead as he inquired, 'Is that you, Farfel?'

'Yes, Bill.'

'What's wrong with it, then?'

'If you give me twenty minutes, I think we can get it right.' And Farfel

146

Grisha Farfel playing a trumpet solo.

A number from Billy Cotton's Music Hall in 1965.

came down from the back and went round to various members of the band. Some twenty minutes later he announced that they were ready.

'All right, Farfel, you take it in,' said Bill, and sat looking away from the band as they struck up. This time everything was just right.

When the number was over Bill turned round, his glasses still on his forehead, and said, 'Farfel, one of these days I'm going to invent a new bleedin' country, and you ain't bleedin' going to be in it.' Which, of course, was his way of complimenting Farfel on doing a good job.

THE CUSSED ENGLISHMAN

The time came when Billy Cotton had to concede that the joke must finally be on him. He died on 25 March 1969 whilst watching a boxing match at Wembley. On the previous night at a charity dinner he had sung 'Maybe It's Because I'm a Londoner' in memory of Bud Flanagan, though, as Bill said, 'It's my song'. Bill Cotton was, in fact, singing his own requiem. And he even spoke his own obituary.

On the morning of the last day of his life he summed up his career. 'I have lived my life as an Englishman: a cussed Englishman sometimes, for when I was warned off playing "There'll Always Be an England" at the Glasgow Empire I still played it. I am as shy as the average Englishman, and as warm as he is when the crust of reserve has been broken. I respond to warmth, and I hope I give it. People say we are not warm-natured any more. In my life I find enough who are.

'My satisfaction has been in seeing people enjoy themselves to my music. Over the years they have danced to it – very seriously and strictly at one time – and they have courted to it. Many a couple still look across the room to each other and say, "That's our tune." All generations have laughed at the show – pleasantly, harmlessly, because I never liked dirty jokes in the parlour. I have given the British public the same courtesy in their own sitting-rooms as I have extended, I hope, to the Royal Family in their palaces.'

But Billy Cotton himself would never allow his biggest Band Show to fade out on a solemn note. And now, to end, a further couple of anecdotes.

Michael Hurll recalls, 'Bill went to Ireland, and he said he was going to play "Land of Hope and Glory" to finish the show. Everybody said, "You don't want to do that in Dublin," and I won't tell you what he said back. On the stage in Dublin, he hoisted a bloody great Union Jack, as wide as the stage, and he played "Land of Hope and Glory". In the interval before the second house a note was delivered to him made up of letters cut out of a newspaper. It said: IF YOU PLAY THAT THE SECOND HOUSE WE WILL

SHOOT YOU and it was signed A FRIEND. "Ah," said Bill, "those buggers aren't going to tell me." So he went on and played the second house, and he finished with "Land of Hope and Glory". Earlier there had been a sharp-shooting act, and the fellow was cleaning his gun just on the side of the stage. There was a round left in it, and suddenly it went off with a hell of a bang. Of course, the band thought that somebody was having a go as promised, and they sprinted off the stage in the middle of "Land of Hope and Glory". And the only man who was left was – Bill Cotton.'

Finally, the 'Cottonism' which probably best sums up all that has been said in this book. During an argument between Bill and the band Bill said, 'Now look 'ere – let's have it understood! There are no exceptions in this band – and no favourites. We're all equal – only *I* just happen to be more equal than the rest of yer!' Well – who would question that!

And so, on a laugh, we end the greatest Billy Cotton Band Show. And don't forget:

Index

Italic references indicate an illustration

153

154

155